UKRAINIAN SHUMKA DANCERS

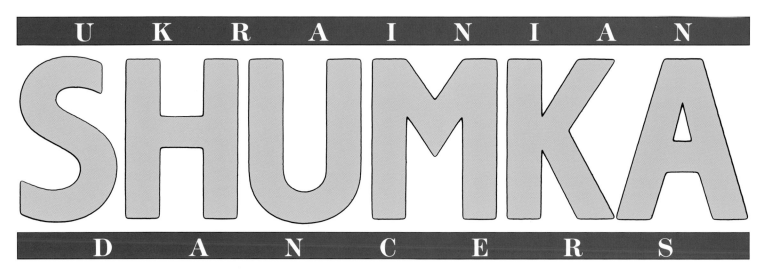

UKRAINIAN
SHUMKA
DANCERS
TRADITION IN MOTION

ШУМКА: ТРАДИЦІЯ В РУСІ

BY: ALICE MAJOR

MANAGING EDITOR: GORDON GORDEY

Reidmore Books Inc.
Edmonton, Alberta
CANADA

Canadian Cataloguing in Publication Data

Major, Alice.

  ISBN 1-895073-01-4

  1. Ukrainian Shumka Dancers. 2. Dance companies—Canada. 3. Folk dancing, Ukrainian—Canada. I. Gordey, Gordon. II. Title.
GV1625.5.A4M34 1991   793.3'1947'71   C91-091439-7

Editorial Committee
MaryAnn Baziuk
Natalka Beaudoin
Annette Bidniak
Betty Corlett
Halyna Elkow
Terry Mucha-Lynn

Copy-Editing
Antoinette Sevensma

Shumka: Tradition in Motion is a project of the Ukrainian Shumka Dancers Alumni Association. The association was officially registered on January 2, 1987, to provide a liaison between ex-members of Shumka and the company. One of the association's goals was to assist the Ukrainian Shumka Dancers in compiling an accurate history of the company.

REIDMORE BOOKS INC.
Suite 012 Lemarchand Mansion
11523 - 100 Avenue
Edmonton, Alberta
CANADA T5K 0J8

printed and bound in Hong Kong

TABLE OF CONTENTS

ACKNOWLEDGEMENTS

Special thanks for their assistance with historical and ethnographic material to:

Radomir Bilash, Senior Research Historian, Ukrainian Cultural Heritage Village,
   Alberta Culture and Multiculturalism,

Dr Andrij Hornjatkevyc, Associate Professor of Slavic and Eastern European Studies,
   University of Alberta,

Dr Andriy Nahachewsky, Huculak Chair of Ukrainian Culture and Ethnography,
   University of Alberta,

Dr E. Joy Muller,

Alberta Cultural Heritage Foundation.

Special thanks also to Ed Ellis, principal photographer.

PREFACE

"Ukrainian dance is an expressive art form. It's not static—it lives and breathes and it goes forward. There are elements in the culture that represent the character and soul of the people, and these don't change. However, the way you express them is open to interpretation and development."

—John Pichlyk

THE LVIV State Opera and Ballet Theatre in western Ukraine, August 20, 1990.

A wave of applause breaks over the dancers posed for their curtain call. They look out at tier upon tier of stalls, boxes, balconies rising up, up, up—until even the allegorical figures painted on the distant ceiling seem to wave and toss down flowers.

Natalie Prytuluk could feel perspiration trailing a river down her spine, down the back of her legs and into her boots. It was torture standing still, listening to the speeches, when she wanted to throw her arms around people and hug them.

This was the last performance in Ukraine. Tomorrow, the dancers would

The ornate splendour of the Lviv State Opera and Ballet Theatre frames the Canadian Shumka Dancers. During the company's 1990 tour of Ukraine, they performed in the finest theatres—a long way from the UNO hall, Edmonton, Alberta where Shumka put on its first concert in 1959.

The magic created for Ukrainian audiences in Enchanted Love used sophisticated stagecraft, costumes, music and choreography to tell a story based on Ukrainian folklore. Members of the company wondered how audiences in the old country would respond to these innovations, but the praise they received was enthusiastic.

fly on to Moscow to give two more concerts. But this was the last time they would appear before an audience in the homeland, where the Ukrainian Shumka Dancers had dreamed of performing for decades.

Shumka came to Ukraine with great eagerness, but also with some anxiety. The company had been founded thirty years earlier, with the goal of preserving a rich Ukrainian dance heritage, in a city half a world away from the Dnipro River. While Shumka remained passionately committed to preserving the authenticity of their Ukrainian heritage, the company was equally passionate about presenting that heritage in new ways.

The concert just completed had told two tales in dance. *Enchanted Love* was a bittersweet story about the interaction between mortals and the complex spirit world of Ukrainian myth. The troupe had used North American theatre techniques such as lighting, stage effects, and costumes to evoke wood nymphs and goblins, and dance techniques from ballet and other disciplines.

They had gone far beyond the simple folk dances of the original village repertoire. Pushing the boundaries had been a painstaking, sometimes painful process, not always accepted by the Ukrainian-Canadian community in Edmonton. How would the people from whom the dance and the myths originated react?

The applause and the speeches went on, warm and reassuring.

"How were you able, in Canada, to portray all of this in its purest form, while we in Ukraine are already forgetting how it was, and is? For this, from our hearts, we thank you."

The words of Lviv's commissioner of culture, himself a poet, put a final stamp of approval on the vigorous applause audiences had offered since the Ukraine tour started. For artistic director John Pichlyk, standing in this theatre less than a hundred miles from his father's birthplace, this approval was immensely important. Shumka had brought its gift to the homeland, and the gift had been accepted.

A TIME OF TRANSITION

Perhaps the events offstage had something to do with the warm welcome. The summer of 1990 was a time of transition all over Eastern Europe as centralized Soviet systems of control broke down. People were jubilant and hungry for new ideas.

Ukrainian flags waved; churches that had been closed for decades were opened. While Shumka was touring Ukraine, statues of Lenin were being taken down in towns and cities around the country, to be replaced by statues of the great Ukrainian poets, Ivan Franko and Taras Shevchenko.

Thirty years earlier, the Shumka dancers had performed at the unveiling of a statue of Taras Shevchenko in Winnipeg, Canada. The long repression of Ukrainian language and culture in the old country had made Ukrainians in Canada feel that they had to preserve their culture in a new land.

The tour, and the events surrounding it, relieved some of that pressure for Shumka's members. Two months before their arrival, Ukrainian sovereignty had

ПРОТОКОЛ НАМІРІВ

між Міністерстом культури УРСР та фірмю "Грейт Вордлд Артистс Лтд". /Канада/

Київ   28 жовтня 1989 р.

В наслідок обговорення питань, пов "язаних з перспективами співробітництва в 1990-1991 році, сторони домовились:

Вивчити можливість організації гастролей в республіці канадського самодіяльного танцювального ансамбля "Шумка" в серпні 1990 року...

Організацією гастролей "Шумка" на Україні буде займатись Республіканска зовнішньоекономічна фірма "Укркультура" при сприянні Міністерства культури УРСР...

Після додаткового вивчення питання організації гастролей "Шумки" на Україні фірма "Укркультура" підпише I січня 1990 року контракт з фірмою "Грейд Бордлд Артистс Лтд".

Від Міністерства культури УРСР   Від фірми "Грейд Ворлд Артустс Лтд"

Перший заступник Міністра
С.В. Колтунюк   Джон Кріптон

A symptom of change: when the final contract for Shumka's Ukraine tour arrived, it was written in Ukrainian, not the Russian of early drafts.

been declared. Throughout the company's negotiations for the tour, documents had arrived written in Russian. Significantly, when the final agreement arrived for signature, it was written in the Ukrainian language.

It was clear to the dancers that the Ukrainian heritage was sturdy; it did not have to be kept safe behind glass with a do-not-touch sign. It was clear that

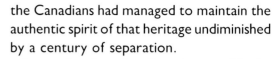

the Canadians had managed to maintain the authentic spirit of that heritage undiminished by a century of separation.

It was also clear that Canadians could take the traditions and the soul of their Ukrainian heritage and make something that speaks in a true voice to both homelands, old and new.

Another symptom of change: Shumka's Ukraine tour took place during a period of intense change in Eastern Europe. Here, a religious procession celebrates Spas (The Transfiguration of the Saviour) *in Lviv. Religious activities had been suppressed for decades.*

For dancers like Taras Stefura, Ukrainian dance is a living, exuberant art form. The spirit that infuses their work is a sturdy flame that leaps from generation-to-generation.

Shumka dancers keep alive traditions that reflect the essence of the homeland and their lives as Canadians of Ukrainian descent. Pryvit—the traditional Ukrainian welcome of bread and salt—is a traditional opening for performances. Pryvit reflects the ancient bond between the Ukrainian people and the rich soil of their homeland. To Shumka it also represents the welcome given to their ancestors by the new land.

CREATING A WHIRLWIND

"...most exciting and dynamic folk dance group in this country . . . Talent, exuberance and polish make them a national treasure."

—John Hirsch, Creative Director and
Producer of Festival Canada's
July 1 Celebrations, 1977

ORIGINS OF SHUMKA

THE YEAR: 1959 . . .

EDMONTON, ALBERTA, 1959—a prairie city of 300 000 souls, hugging the banks of the North Saskatchewan, 300 miles north of the 49th parallel.

International politics were dominated by the Cold War—atomic bomb testing, Soviet President Nikita Krushchev arriving in the USA to visit President Eisenhower, the race between superpowers to get men into space.

Nevertheless, 1959 was a period of prosperity and stability for Canada. Employment across the country was at a post-war high of 96.5 per cent. The biggest complaint from voters was a tight money policy that sent interest rates climbing to 6.75 per cent.

Shumka preserves and recreates the pride and desire for freedom that the first Ukrainian immigrants brought with them to Canada.

Queen Elizabeth opened the St. Lawrence Seaway; the Montreal Canadiens defeated the Toronto Maple Leafs to win a fourth straight Stanley Cup. Edmonton did not yet have a National Hockey League team, but it did have Canada's first double-decker parking garage.

Alberta was riding an oil development boom that had started early in the decade. The province had money to spend—and spent it. Edmonton's Jubilee Auditorium had been completed a year or two earlier to celebrate the fiftieth anniversary of Alberta becoming a province. It was the twin sister to the Jubilee Auditorium in Calgary, and in 1959, one of the highlights on Edmonton's Jubilee stage was a travelling production of *My Fair Lady*.

Around the world, dance was experiencing a postwar revival and Canada was beginning to put together its own dance institutions. The National Ballet of Canada had been established eight years earlier, with Edmonton-trained Grant Strate as one of its founding dancers. Out west, to the surprise of many, the Royal Winnipeg Ballet's energetic Arnold Spohr had increased the company's season to include forty-two performances presented to audiences totalling 33 000 people.

In 1959, dance in Canada was a fledgling art form—a combination of imported culture and a newly stirring ambition to create a sense of the country in music and movement.

THE UKRAINIAN COMMUNITY

Edmonton's population in 1959 was a mix of Scots, English, German and a variety of people from Central Europe who had come to settle the Prairies. Approximately 35 000 citizens were Canadians of Ukrainian origin.

Edmonton's Ukrainian community was by no means a homogeneous group in 1959. Several waves of immigrants had arrived since the first Ukrainian settlers reached Canada in 1891. Each group had its own religious beliefs and political convictions, its own motives for leaving the homeland— that fertile land, which had been invaded and dominated by foreign powers for more than a thousand years. Each had its own experience of the new country, Canada.

The first wave of immigrants arrived during the two decades before World War I, encouraged by a Canadian government that was anxious to populate the empty lands of western Canada. They came primarily from the western Ukraine regions of Halychyna and Bukovyna, then under the Austro-Hungarian Empire. The newcomers left behind them a country racked by social and economic upheaval. With the abolition of serfdom in 1848, wealthy landowners had demanded compensation for loss of ancient privileges. Farmers were burdened by debt, and their tiny farm holdings had been subdivided by successive generations into impossibly small units. Halychyna had the lowest income and highest mortality rates in the Austro-Hungarian Empire.

Ukrainian immigrant children, circa 1907. The first wave of Ukrainian immigrants to Canada reached a peak in the late 1890s, as people came seeking freedom and opportunities for their children. They found freedom, but also endured great hardship in the early years.

One link in the chain binding peasants to this difficult life was widespread illiteracy. In response, a new village institution arose in the last quarter of the century: the **chytalnia**, or reading club. Peasants met in the *chytalnia* on Sundays and holidays to hear literate villagers read from newspapers, booklets, and pamphlets. They learned about politics and agriculture—and they learned about opportunities to settle overseas.

In 1891, two Ukrainians, Ivan Pylypow and Wasyl Eleniak, came to Canada to investigate settlement opportunities in the West. But the real mass immigration to Canada began in 1896, accelerated by the work of a young agronomist, Dr Joseph Oleskiw. His pamphlets, *About Free Lands* and *On Emigration* were widely read and discussed in the reading clubs.

In Canada, the Ukrainian immigrants took up the government's offer of 160 acres for the sum of $10. Many settled in the aspen parklands north and east of Edmonton, establishing the oldest and largest Ukrainian settlement on the Prairies. By spring, 1904, there were 16 000 Ukrainians on 2500 homesteads in east-central Alberta.

They took up the task of breaking stubborn ground, often surviving their first winters in various types of dug-out dwellings. Life was exceptionally hard. Their dress and language set them apart from their neighbours and the inevitable ethnic slurs were used like weapons.

Though there was little time or energy to spare, many a homestead cabin had a violin or **tsymbaly** hanging in the corner. The songs of the old country soothed sleepy children, cheered community gatherings, and preserved the stories and language of the old country.

The second wave of immigrants brought another 68 000 Ukrainians to Canada after World War I. These Ukrainians were generally better-educated than their predecessors. They were political and economic refugees, carrying a flame of revived nationalism in their hearts. Although Ukraine had been carved into four pieces as a result of the war, a rise in Ukrainian self-awareness had been created by the disintegration of the Austro-Hungarian Empire, the overthrow of the tsarist government, and other political developments. Some of these immigrants felt the destroyers of the tsarist empire were freeing Ukraine from oppression and joined pro-Soviet organizations in Canada.

The third wave of immigrants came after World War II. This group consisted almost exclusively of political refugees and soldiers who had escaped through Europe to North America. Many of them had spent time in camps for displaced persons.

These post-World War II refugees included well-educated urban painters, musicians, and scholars who had been intellectual and cultural leaders in their home communities. Most came from Russian-dominated areas of Ukraine. They were militantly anti-communist, embittered by Stalinist policies.

With them, they brought a tremendous longing to ensure that Ukrainian culture was preserved, even if it had to be preserved in Canada rather than in the homeland. The early settlers had brought traditional dances that they practised primarily as a social diversion. As a result of the new immigrants, additional dances were being taught all over the country as a symbol of identity with Ukraine and pride in its heritage.

By 1959, members of the Ukrainian community in Edmonton were playing leading roles in business, in civic and provincial politics, and in education. They identified strongly with the old country, but they were also anxious to take their place on the Canadian stage and were proud of the advancements their community was making. One Ukrainian newspaper announced with delight the appointment of John Hnatyshyn, QC, to the Canadian Senate:

"His choice by Prime Minister Diefenbaker as the first of his race in Saskatchewan to go to the Senate is a recognition of the great role Canadian Ukrainians have played and are continuing to play in this growing country."

The community was still characterized by deep divisions, including political ideology. For many, their early socialist sympathies had been confirmed by the hardships of the Depression and the appalling working conditions in the mines where so many Ukrainian immigrants found work. At the same time, news of the Stalinist terrors in Soviet Ukraine, combined with their own experiences of World War II, convinced many others that communism was a sworn enemy of Ukrainian culture.

The enthusiasm for communism in Canada had reached its peak in the late 1940s, then went into a decline from which it has never recovered. Religious

The sheepskin coat is a symbol of warmth, pride, and the security that Ukrainian immigrants hoped to find in their new land.

The second wave of Ukrainian immigrants brought 68 000 people to Canada during the years after World War I. They were political and economic refugees, in whom the war and its aftermath had created a strong awareness of their identity as Ukrainians. Here, passengers improvise a **kolomyika** *on one of the Canada-bound steamships of 1921. Photo: United Church of Canada/Victoria University Archives, Toronto.*

differences among Russian Orthodox, Ukrainian Orthodox, and Ukrainian Catholic members of the community remained strong in the late 1950s—although there were signs that this division, too, was beginning to break down.

An organization known as the Ukrainian National Federation (UNO) had been founded in Edmonton in 1932, and subsequently spread to other parts of Canada. Edmonton's UNO hall was built in 1948 and was intended to become a focus of unity for all Ukrainians, whether Catholic or Orthodox.

By 1959, the various sectors of Edmonton's Ukrainian community did share one important common denominator: pride in their heritage.

The early settlers had taken a stubborn pride in their Ukrainian roots, but were aware that it often brought them only scorn and intolerance from their Canadian neighbours. However, by the 1950s, the first immigrants had earned solid economic success and respect for their capabilities. Newer immigrants added an awareness that Ukrainian culture could be a source of intellectual pride. Ukrainians began to feel they could put forward their culture not only as a personal expression but also as a valued offering to the larger Canadian community.

Dance was becoming an increasingly popular expression of this cultural pride. In 1960, the Yevshan Dancers were founded in Saskatoon to offer young people "the opportunity of learning Ukrainian folk dancing in its most aesthetic form." In Winnipeg, the Rusalka Ukrainian Dance Ensemble was formed in 1962. Both groups went on to perform for audiences nationally and internationally.

Nowhere was the urge to use dance as an expression of Ukrainian culture stronger than in Edmonton, where the Ukrainian Shumka Dancers emerged in 1959.

SHUMKA—THE WHIRLWIND BEGINS

In the mid-1950s, several Ukrainian dance groups were active in Edmonton. Shumka emerged from an amalgam of their talents, pushed by the overriding vision of one young man, Chester Kuc.

The two primary groups were based at the St. John's Ukrainian Orthodox Cathedral on 107th Street and at the UNO hall on 98th Street. The St. John's dance group had been organized in 1952, with Vera Zaputovich as instructor. Kuc took over from her in 1956, and by 1958 was teaching at the UNO hall as well, so there was considerable overlap between the two groups.

Other organizations such as the Ukrainian Youth Association (SUM) were also working to promote the community's heritage. SUM sponsored the Ukrainian Youth Camp in 1958 where dance was a major activity under the instruction of Michael Horban. And at St. Josaphat's Ukrainian Catholic Cathedral, a young woman called Luba Stangret was continuing to practise and perform the dances she had learned while in a displaced persons camp in Germany.

Chester Kuc had a vision of putting together a "supergroup" of Ukrainian dancers to perform on a large scale. One motivation was the fact that, as his young students at the UNO hall and St. John's reached their late teens, they had nowhere to go when it came to Ukrainian dancing.

"We were at a standstill. We weren't going anywhere with our dancing," he recalls. He was also driven by a desire to outdo the performances sponsored by communist organizations during the 1940s and early 1950s. In particular, a series of Taras Shevchenko concerts put on by the communist Association of United Ukrainian Canadians throughout the late 1950s was considered an affront by nationalist Ukrainians. Kuc wanted to see the nationalists "pull off one major concert" that was bigger and better than anything done before.

He spotted Luba Stangret during a duet she performed in 1958 to celebrate the tenth anniversary of the Alberta Ukrainian Catholic Eparchy, and drew her into his plans. Stangret was an attractive, talented, and devoutly Catholic young woman with some very decided ideas about the terms on which she would join any new group. She stipulated that there should be no affiliation with a political/religious organization, that rehearsals would be held on neutral ground, and that membership would be open to all on the basis of their interest and ability.

This decision to cross the boundaries of tradition and organizational loyalties did not go entirely unopposed in a deeply traditional community. "Our independent dancing group has started a bit of controversy or opposition by people from the church, as this is a

The first dancers joined Shumka for many reasons, including pride in their heritage, the thrill of performing, and the simple teenage desire to have fun. This photo was taken in 1960, shortly after Shumka's founding. Back row, from left: Martha Pawluk, Khrystyna Yopuk, Rose Klapey, Darlene Kassian, Irene Warnick, Pat Pelech, Lesia Yusypchuk, Betty Pelech, Nona Pylipiuk, Kathy Rhodes, Marsha Weleschuk, Sven Izio, Audrey Kuzyk, Natalka Dobrolige, Dianne Kassian, Lois Sulyma, Mary Hoshko. Front row: Mike Klapey, Don Palylyk, Leonard Wasylynchuk, Gerry Metrunec, Leo Zalucky, Terry Sulyma, Levern Wasylynchuk, Toby Eshenko, Taras Semchuk. Photo: Alpha Studio (J. Fedoriw)

Wadym Dobrolige's carefully painted sets framed Shumka's early performances, such as this 1962 concert in Edmonton's Jubilee Auditorium. Photo: Academy Studio (J. Prima).

mixed group of dancers from all of the youth clubs and some don't like it," Kuc wrote to his fiancée in the early months.

In spite of the controversy, the Shumka dancers started to gather momentum. Members were specifically invited to join on the basis of their talent, and sometimes on the basis of gender. It was hard to drum up enough males to match the number of females. One of the founding dancers, Leo Zalucky, joined at first on a dare, and stayed only because he "liked the looks of one of the girls."

The first rehearsals took place late in 1958. Over the next year or so, membership fluctuated dramatically. Many of the dancers were active young people who were leaders in school clubs, sports teams, and community groups, so conflicts existed between the demands of school and the commitment to the concept of extensive performances envisioned by Kuc.

Nevertheless, the fledgling troupe stuck together sufficiently to compete in the Canada-wide UNO competitions in Saskatoon in April. The group presented its first concert on November 29, 1959 at the UNO hall.

The second concert took place in February 1960 in the basement of St. John's Cathedral. Within three months, Shumka was presenting its first major concert at the Jubilee Auditorium for an audience of 1200 people. The group's size of twenty-one dancers established Shumka's trademark swirl of massed colours right from the beginning.

For these early performances, Stangret functioned as co-instructor, director, and choreographer. Wadym Dobrolige began his long commitment to providing elaborately painted sets and acting as stage manager. An enthusiastic group of parents devoted many hours to ensure the authenticity of the costumes.

Kuc was in charge of organization and took the lion's share of responsibility. One of his early priorities was to find guest artists to keep interest high among dancers and audiences. The program for the October 1960 concert at the Jubilee included the Yevshan Dancers from Saskatoon and Taras Semchuk ("a young man who has just returned from two years' study at the Royal Ballet School in London, England.")

The early members of Shumka reflected the history of the Ukrainian community in Canada. Some were already third- and fourth-generation descendants of

the first wave of settlers. For example, Gerry Metrunec's great-grandfather, Simon Dmytronetz had settled in Pathfinder, Alberta in 1896. Others reflected more recent arrivals: Luba Stangret, for instance, lived in a displaced persons camp until 1951.

The early dancers like Orest Yusypchuk, Levern Wasylynchuk, and Sylvia Lytwin often joined for social reasons—motivations typical of any North American teenager of the time. Many did see themselves as representatives of "free" Ukraine, trying to present the best of their heritage. But as much as anything else, they wanted to dance "for the fun of it."

None of them realized that the energy they released in those early rehearsals would still be going strong three decades later.

UKRAINIAN DANCE:

Roots in the Old Country, Branches in the New

THE LINKS BETWEEN HISTORY AND DANCE

Dance is closely bound up with the history of the people who dance it. Ukrainian dance is inextricably linked to the turbulent history of its fertile homeland—a country that straddles the dividing line between Eastern and Western Europe and whose political borders have been drawn and re-drawn many times.

By the fifth and sixth centuries, several Slavic tribes were living in what is now Ukraine. They became the forerunners of the ethnolinguistic group known as Ukrainians, a term that first appeared in the twelfth century. Eventually, one of these Slavic tribes decided to accept support from the Varangians, a Viking group, against pressure from the Khazar Empire to the east.

Out of this alliance came the gradual unification of the Eastern Slavs and a new state structure known as Kyivan Rus. Kyivan Rus' culture blossomed between the ninth and eleventh centuries, nourished by a rich network of trade links that stretched from the Gulf of Finland to Constantinople. In 988, the Eastern version of Christianity was adopted as the state religion of Kyivan Rus, bringing an important thread into Ukrainian society.

By the thirteenth century, however, Kyivan Rus was

under siege. In 1240, Tatar hordes sacked Kyiv and the fertile lands of Ukraine became the stage for an all-too-frequent drama of invasion and domination, first by Tatars, and later by Lithuanians, Poles, and Muscovites.

The constant threat of invasion prompted the rise of an important group in Ukrainian society—the **kozaky**. By the 1620s, the *kozaky* were proclaiming themselves as defenders of the Orthodox people of Ukraine. Their military success was sufficient to establish a *kozak* state that survived in various forms until 1775.

Over the centuries, the descendants of Kyivan Rus watched tides of invasion come and go. They lived primarily in rural agricultural communities, in a feudal society where serfdom was not abolished until the middle of the nineteenth century. They tilled the soil, married and gave birth, while the lives of their various rulers went on disconnected from them.

And they danced.

DANCE: *Roots in Religion*

In the earliest Ukrainian societies, as in most cultures, dance was not entertainment or artistic expression. Instead, it was a spiritual matter, closely intertwined with the cycle of the year, the growing of crops, the solemn transitions of life. People danced so that the grain would grow tall and the sun return from its low point on the winter horizon.

Several manifestations of this ancient tradition have come down to our time. These *khorovody* are usually slow, rhythmic, and repetitive, often composed of a circle or chain of singers holding hands and walking.

With the emergence of Kyivan Rus culture, dance took on new functions. Lighter, livelier dances accompanied by instrumental music were added. The directly religious character of the old pagan dances was cloaked and modified by the influence of the church; the celebrations of the winter solstice became absorbed into the festival of the birth of Christ and midsummer celebrations were re-dedicated to St. John.

In early cultures, all members of the tribe participated in the dance. The increasing sophistication of Kyivan Rus culture brought about another innovation—the split between audience and performer.

The first semi-professional artists were the **skomorokhy**. Their repertoire was based on folk song, puppetry, juggling, and dance, but they performed in the prince's court, as well as wandering from village to village to play for merchant and peasant alike. Dance appeared in a new context. The new dances had to be geared for viewers, not performers. Spectacle became an important consideration, with energetic leaps, acrobatics, and lively patterns. Comedy became another important element. Themes were usually humourous and movements exaggerated.

The downfall of the Kyivan Rus Empire put an end to the arts of the *skomorokhy* in Ukraine. Over subsequent generations, Ukrainian dance turned in on itself and became primarily a recreational form in an era of true folk art—art that is significant in social and recreational aspects rather than in its religious or theatrical nature.

Ukrainian folk dance evolved for centuries in relative isolation from the influence of court or "art" dance. Folk dance expressed the basic round of peasant life.

Court dance never evolved in Ukraine to the degree it did in Italy or France, where lively folk traditions were transformed into the stately *pavane* or the lighter *gavotte*. In Ukraine, the aristocracy were generally foreigners by origin and seldom shared the interests of the people they ruled. In other parts of Europe, the energy of folk dance was compressed into the rigid patterns of court dance before diffusing into new genres like ballet. In Ukraine, where folk culture remained for much longer, dance continued to reflect the cycle of agricultural life.

DANCE: A Political Statement

The closeness to daily life was a factor as Ukrainian dance developed and emerged as a conscious symbol of national identity.

Centuries of foreign domination had suppressed but not quenched the Ukrainians' sense of themselves as a people with a much-loved language and heritage. The rich variety of music and folk dance that evolved during generations of relative isolation played an important role in helping self-awareness survive through the centuries.

In the fifteenth century, Ukrainian culture had been in serious eclipse. Four centuries later, the infamous tsarist memorandum of 1863 declared that the Ukrainian language did not, and never had existed. However, the suppressed culture continually welled up between the fingers of the oppressors. By the 1880s a major cultural reawakening was underway. Folk culture moved into the theatre, where plays saturated with ethnography and the romanticized life of the Ukrainian people became wildly popular.

The old concerns of spectacle and entertainment value of the *skomorokhy* were resurrected in the new theatrical performances. The climax of most was the **hopak**, an acrobatic dance that showcased massed displays of dancers and individual virtuosity.

Theatrical entrepreneurs mounted spectacular performances and toured them as far as St. Petersburg. Some reviewers bewailed the "cult of the *hopak*," in which literary quality of the dramas was swamped entirely by the dazzle of the dance. But to most members of the audience, the theatrical performances spoke to a deep need for pride in themselves and their heritage.

Inevitably, the move from village to stage changed folk dance in subtle but fundamental ways. Dancers were not doing real folk dances, but were consciously recreating them in a proscenium setting. These staged dances were oriented to a front, the vantage point of the audience. The choreography was purposely modified and polished to intensify energy and vitality. Dance compositions were made more complex, which required changes in dance training, research, and in related theatrical skills. But primarily, it involved a change in attitude. Dance had become a symbol of national identity, and spread to the politically active intelligentsia emerging in Ukraine's growing cities. Peasants and villagers had danced to express life and happiness. On stage, actors danced because it was Ukrainian—and because the audiences enjoyed it.

In spite of these important developments in the form and motivation for dancing, the basic vocabulary of movement and dance forms remained unchanged. The dance as a whole remained essentially populist—an art form accessible to ordinary people, rather than highly formalized and abstract. Most importantly, the dance remained Ukrainian. It took on newly intensified symbolic connotations, but to the people watching and responding, the dance was *theirs*.

THE CROSSING TO CANADA

The earliest wave of Ukrainian settlers in Alberta brought their dances to the new land: the *kolomyika*, where dancers formed a moving circle with individuals moving into the centre of the circle to do solo improvisations, and the **hutsulka**. Dancing was primarily a social activity, a diversion stolen from the hours of labour of breaking soil and feeding families. There was no formal instruction, so steps and musical melodies were improvised from the memories of the old country. Contact with other Canadians modified social patterns and western social dances began to replace the traditional heritage to some degree.

The second, post-World War I wave of immigrants brought staged Ukrainian dance to North America. They also brought a heightened awareness of the possibility that Ukraine could become a nation independent of foreign domination. They had lived through the turbulent war years and the overthrow of the tsarist government. They had seen the formation of the short-lived Ukrainian Democratic Republic, declared in 1917 and replaced in 1921 by a Bolshevik-led Soviet Ukrainian government.

One of the most influential figures in the history of Ukrainian dance lived through this period of upheaval before coming to Canada in 1925. His name was Vasile Avramenko.

AVRAMENKO: *Founder of Ukrainian Dance in Canada*

Avramenko studied theatre at the Mykola Lysenko drama school in Kyiv, where he met Professor Vasyl Verkhovynets, the first scholar to research and publish a manual on Ukrainian dance. Avramenko's career as actor and dancer was interrupted by his country's fight for independence. He volunteered for the army but was told by the Ukrainian leader, Symon Petliura, that he would do more for the national cause on the stage than with a gun.

He toured with a theatre group from 1918 to 1921, until the collapse of the republic threw him into an internment camp in Poland. He promptly began to teach Ukrainian dance at the camp. He organized a small troupe that was able to tour western Ukraine for a while before being ordered back to the internment camp by Polish authorities.

Avramenko managed to go on teaching and organizing dance classes in Ukrainian schools throughout the parts of western Ukraine under Polish and Czechoslovakian rule. Finally, in 1925, he decided to come to North America.

On this side of the Atlantic, he immediately established his first school in Toronto. In barely eight months, he had a hundred dancers performing at the Canadian National Exhibition and created a genuine sensation among the spectators.

Throughout the 1920s and early 1930s, he travelled from city to city, first in Canada and then in the United States, to set up schools and teach his dances. In 1935, he turned his attention to film-making. In the 1940s and for the rest of his long career he gave workshops and organized concerts around the world, from Australia to Israel.

Avramenko put a definite stamp on Ukrainian dance in the first half of the century. He had absorbed Verkhovynets' dictum that folk dance should be presented in its pure form—a reaction to the strenuous acrobatics that had become a focus of many theatre groups in Ukraine.

He worked from a curriculum of eighteen dances that he had collected between 1919 and 1924. Steps and formations were relatively simple, to allow great numbers of people to learn them in a short time. An entire dance would usually consist of ten dance figures. In turn, each figure consisted of one or more steps repeated for eight or sixteen bars of music. Although he admitted to occasionally rearranging old dances and choreographing new ones, he continued to assert that Ukrainian dance should be presented in its original form.

Linked to his passion for authenticity was his sense

Life was exceptionally hard for the immigrants who first settled western Canada and breaking the land took most of their time and energy. However, when they could celebrate together, their love of dance and music re-emerged. Here, immigrants in Alberta take part in an outdoor festivity circa 1902.

of dance as a symbol of nationhood. For him, dance represented the heroism forged by Ukraine's long history and the conviction of ultimate freedom. It was a political weapon.

''The dance is a language, a powerful language by which we communicate from the soul . . . The Ukrainian dance is a threat to our neighbours, who wish to rule over our nation. They don't want the Ukrainian soul to speak, to live, to be free and strong,'' he would say in his numerous speeches.

Avramenko toured western Canada in August and in the autumn of 1927 with a group of dancers chosen from his school in Winnipeg, reaching many Ukrainian Canadians who had never before seen their national dances performed on a stage. The excitement caused by the performances soon had Ukrainian communities throughout the Prairies clamouring for their own schools.

Edmonton had already established a school, following an earlier visit by Avramenko in March, 1926. Using his well established pattern, he had taught a series of dances from his core curriculum, then had his students put on a final concert at the Empire Theatre.

He returned to Edmonton on several occasions over the next three decades and influenced the founding members of Shumka either directly or indirectly. Luba Stangret recalled that he would often stay with her family when he visited the city. Several of the founding members, including Zoria and Sylvia Lytwin and Len

Vasile Avramenko created enormous interest in Ukrainian dance in North America after he arrived in 1925. A passionate Ukrainian nationalist, he saw dance as a symbol of nationhood and collected a repertoire of dances that could be taught to hundreds, even thousands, of children and adults in a relatively short time. Here, members of the first school of Ukrainian dance in Vegreville, Alberta pose after a performance in 1928. Their performance was directed by one of Avramenko's principal teachers, Ivan Pihuliak. Photo: Provincial Archives of Alberta.

Avramenko's influence spread quickly throughout western Canada. His repertoire of folk dances, collected mostly from villages in central Ukraine, became the basis for most of the dances taught across Canada. Here, boys perform an **arkan** in the community of Vilna, Alberta in 1929.

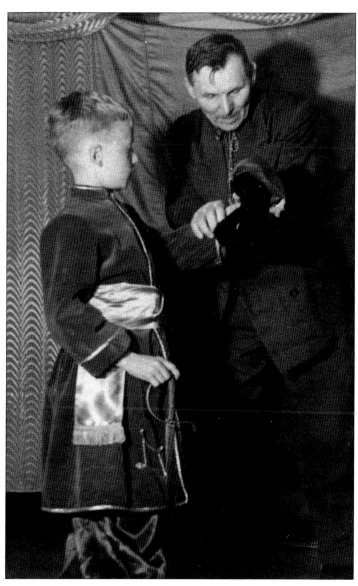

Vasile Avramenko was a frequent visitor to Edmonton and directly influenced many of the early members of Shumka. Here, he is photographed in 1951 with Taras Semchuk, brother of artistic-director-to-be Orest Semchuk.

and Levern Wasylynchuk, were products of Avramenko's certificate program. At the concluding concert of Avramenko's 1956-57 course at the UNO Hall, one of the featured performers in the *Sword Dance* was Chester Kuc.

AFTER AVRAMENKO

Vasile Avramenko was undoubtedly the father of Ukrainian folk dance in North America. But by the 1940s, some people were becoming frustrated by certain limitations of his approach. Choreographers began introducing new elements to the traditional repertoire. Dancers waited eagerly for rare visits by touring Soviet companies—or equally rare film footage of their performances—in order to expand their vocabulary of steps and techniques. Tours by Moscow's Moiseyev Dance Company in 1958 and 1961, and the Virsky Ukrainian State Ensemble in 1962 and 1966, demonstrated new standards of technical excellence.

To a large extent, Ukrainian dance in Canada has developed in isolation from its roots over the past six decades. Printed material was not accessible, research in the area was still limited, and contacts with Ukrainian sources were rare.

Ukrainian dance in Canada has evolved as the community has evolved. Most dancers are now third- or fourth-generation Canadians; to them, Ukraine is very far away. Their motives for dancing are different from Avramenko's flaming desire to promote his country's independence. The joy of performing for an audience, the theatrical experience, and the social opportunities most likely motivate Ukrainian dancers today.

Nevertheless, the primary motivation for most dancers remains what it has always been: to express and share a cultural identity; to say gladly, "I am Ukrainian."

PROFILE: Chester Kuc

When Chester Kuc initiated Shumka in 1959, he was a tall, almost gangling 28-year-old with horn-rimmed glasses that gave him an air of accountant-like earnestness.

He was working in the Court House for the Attorney General's Department and also maintaining a high level of commitment to Ukrainian cultural activities all over the city: the UNO hall, the Ukrainian Catholic National Hall, St. Basil's Ukrainian Catholic Parish, Holy Eucharist Ukrainian Catholic Parish, St. John's Orthodox Cathedral and St. Elia's Ukrainian Orthodox Parish.

Born in Edmonton, Kuc had taken some early dance training from Avramenko and had also studied violin and piano. He was intense, a perfectionist and, above all, someone with a vision.

"I don't like doing anything on a small scale," he says.

On a big scale he wanted to pull together the best Ukrainian dancers in the town—and he taught most of them—to put on one really big performance.

He was an ardent supporter of Ukrainian nationalism. It was a belief that ran in the family. His father was intensely supportive of ambitions to "do better than the communists."

"My dad even offered to put up the money to get us there (to the first performance at the Jubilee Auditorium)," he recalls.

Even ardent nationalists had qualms about whether the new group could indeed pull off such a big endeavour. When 1200 people poured into the Jubilee Auditorium the sense of triumph was mixed with relief and a certain element of "we told you so" for Chester and his young dancers.

Kuc laid down many of the essential traditions of Shumka, such as the use of live music as an accompaniment and the inclusion of guest artists to broaden audience appeal. In his thirties, he started taking ballet classes when he was convinced that ballet techniques could help the presentation of Ukrainian dance. "I was really too old," he recalls ruefully.

But the most basic traditions established by Kuc were his passionate commitment to the preservation of the Ukrainian heritage, and his uncompromising quest for the highest possible standards.

He appreciated that dance was one of the most accessible ways of communicating that heritage and wanted to make sure the message got across to audiences, loudly and clearly.

"Dance attracts people . . . . You don't have to speak the language to enjoy it."

His drive created an inner tension that surfaced from time to time.

"You never knew when he was going to blow up," recalls one dancer. "But we learned a lot."

"You worried for and with him," remembers another.

Shumka came into existence because of Kuc's personal vision, drive, and energy. His pride in the company's achievement still stands. "You were part of it, did it together, brought out something fantastic."

Chester Kuc provided much of the momentum that led to the founding of Shumka. He was inspired by a vision of using dance to express Ukrainian nationalism.

Chester Kuc (front, centre) taught this class at the UNO hall, photographed shortly before the founding of Shumka. Many of these dancers went on to become part of the new group. Back row, from left: Zoria Robinson, Lil Dorash, Daria Kowalchuk, unidentified, Ann Balke, Betty Bartko, Mary Zalucky, Sylvia Shewciw. Front row: Levern Wasylynchuk, Gerald Metrunec, Chester Kuc, Leonard Wasylynchuk, Fred Hladun. Photo, Alpha Studio (J. Fedoriw).

TELLING TALES

"Shumka portrays dance at is best. The company has a young artistic talent of great brilliance . . . a brilliance usually seen only in the most magnificent ballet productions. These dancers perform from the heart and soul."

—Yuri Vrashkin, Virsky Ukrainian
State Dance Company, 1990

THE EVOLUTION OF STORY-LINES

OVER THE YEARS, Shumka's choreography has been shaped by two strong and frequently opposing forces. One is the pressure for authenticity. The group was formed to express and preserve a valued Ukrainian heritage and that motivation remains as important today as it was in 1959.

The second force is the drive for creativity and artistic innovation, a stream that rises from several sources. One is the need to keep highly motivated people interested and challenged by what they do. Another is the need to keep audiences interested and challenged by what they see on stage. The troupe has always taken the goal of creativity seriously. Entertainment is anything

Shumka's distinctive story-line approach to dance theatre brings Ukrainian folklore alive, as in this scene from The Calling.

but a trivial consideration for the people who create a Shumka concert.

The forces of authenticity and creativity have found their expression in an art form that members of the troupe refer to as "story-lines."

WHAT IS A STORY-LINE?

A story-line is similar to the narrative that holds a ballet together. The basic principles for creating such a narrative were recorded more than two centuries ago by the French choreographer Noverre, after ballet had evolved into an art form separate from opera. He stipulated such concepts as, "All ballets should possess a good plot that the audience can follow without program notes."

Noverre's basic principles for telling story through dance are essentially the same as those developed by Shumka for story-lines. Over the years, Shumka's narratives have evolved from simple beginnings to detailed tales with complex plots, rich characters, and immense audience appeal. They provide an opportunity to express a wide range of emotions— humour, mystery, longing and loss—more directly than the more abstract patterns of traditional dance allow. As a result, story-lines permit choreographers to shift pace and mood, keeping audiences involved.

Story-lines also provide a context for the dances themselves. Based on stories, legends and folk traditions of Ukraine, they help an audience understand how dance fitted into daily life and how it reflected social patterns and folk traditions.

To accommodate Shumka's story-line approach, forty-five dancers play a total of 260 character roles and make more than 275 costume changes during a single performance.

THE STORY OF STORY-LINES

Early Shumka concerts were built around the basic dance repertoire taught by Vasile Avramenko. (See page 11.) The program from a 1960 concert consists almost entirely of a list of dances, among them *hopak*, *arkan*, and *kolomyika*.

The constraints of a limited repertoire with simple steps and formations were soon felt. Chester Kuc was a fierce partisan of authenticity. However, he did feel the pressure for change. He had been influenced as a teenager by visits to Winnipeg to take UNO-sponsored summer courses with the active Ukrainian cultural community. In particular, he saw a Ukrainian Folk Ballet, *Krynytsia*, by an American choreographer, and dances staged by Winnipeg's Peter Hladun.

"This sort of opened my eyes. I saw that these people were getting away from the same old routine . . . it was refreshing," he recalls.

The hand-picked group of dancers that formed Shumka included the best dancers in the city at the time. Inevitably, that meant a group of motivated, creative people who were willing to push the borders. At the same time, Canadian dance as a whole was beginning to find its feet as choreographers across the country began to create works of their own. In 1966, Canada's first full-length indigenous ballet, *Rose Latulippe*, was produced, created by Brian Macdonald of the Royal Winnipeg Ballet.

The seeds of the story-line appeared on Shumka programs almost immediately after the group was formed. The 1960 program included a "Ukrainian Folk Ballet" by Taras Semchuk, brother of artistic director-to-be, Orest Semchuk.

One program item in the 1964 concert at the Jubilee Auditorium was *Under the Cherry Tree*, choreographed by Natalka Dobrolige. Here we see the rudiments of fictional characters beginning to develop. Dobrolige herself danced the part of the girl; Orest Semchuk danced the part of the old man. Similarly, on the 1966 program appears *A Kozak Goes to War*, choreographed by Orest Semchuk and Eugene Zwozdesky. The girl was danced by Helen Stechishin; the *kozak* by Zwozdesky.

By the company's tenth anniversary in 1969, the variation in pace and mood had become pronounced in these vignettes, as the following description of *The Dream* demonstrates:

> "The mood is quiet and peaceful. The day has been long but the Eve of St. John promises excitement. A young girl, in love, is tired from the day's preparations and falls asleep. Like all young girls, in her dreams she relives the precious moments with her loved one.

Villagers mock the old husband as he searches for his young wife in Under the Cherry Tree. *Early story-lines were generally brief, almost fragmentary. However they began the development of characterization and plot that later flowered into complex stories that last for half of a Shumka performance.*

Over the years, Shumka's choreography has expanded beyond the presentation of staged folk dance to the telling of fully developed stories through dance. Elements of this story-line approach were evident early in the company's development. Here, in the 1964 performance of Under the Cherry Tree, *Levern Wasylynchuk teases Natalka Dobrolige to come to the village square and dance.*

As in ballet narratives, Shumka's story-lines express emotion through the development of character. Here, Marilyn Mucha weeps over her daughter's blindness in a 1984 performance of A Mother's Tears.
Photo: Bill McKeown.

As story-lines developed, they posed new theatrical challenges to express the magic of Ukrainian legends. Here, Lorrie Sulyma plays Malanka, in a 1982 performance. As the New Year approaches, animals assume human qualities and help select Malanka, the maid of the New Year, who also personifies the coming of spring.

Suddenly she is awakened by her handsome kozak. They are not alone for long. The girls come for her. The celebration has begun. Her heart rejoices."

The simple plot had become more elaborate by 1971, when Shumka performed *Circle*:

"One peaceful day, the girls of one group are seen playing happily before settling down to the daily washing. Gradually their men come to join them and all is normal, with the notable exception of one stranger amidst the girls. The men soon notice her and begin vying for her attention—all to no avail, for she has long ago fallen in love with one of them.

The couple's moments together are few, for suddenly the men of the girl's group appear, strike down her lover and abduct the other women, thus provoking a battle.

While the men prepare for the ensuing struggle and the women mourn over it . . ."

By the mid-1970s, story-line arrangements like *Communion* were taking up almost one-half of a concert. Parallel developments were taking place in other Ukrainian dance groups, notably the Saskatchewan group, Yevshan, which created particularly sophisticated performances throughout the 1960s.

Shumka's early story-lines were based on re-enactments of traditional village ceremonies. In *Harvest* (1973), reapers choose to dance rather than work until the *hospodar*, or landlord, appears; the girls make a wreath of wheat and a harvest queen is chosen to lead the workers to the *hospodar's* house; the landowner greets villagers with bread and salt.

Characters were more or less generic and their motivations could easily be summarized in a phrase or two—girl in love, carefree lumberjacks, teasing boy. Plots were equally straightforward. Basically, plots provided a framework for individual dances rather than standing on their own as stories.

By 1984 the story-line had taken a leap into new realms. The narrative, *A Mother's Tears*, had complex characters, dramatic special effects, and a structured plot in which the dancing reinforced the themes and enhanced characterization. A mysterious traveller visits a village and casts a spell of blindness on one of its maidens, who is only cured through her mother's grief.

A Mother's Tears formed one half of the 1984 concert; the second half was taken up by another story-line, *The Calling*. (See below.) In 1987, the concert tour once again featured two story-lines: *The Travelling Chumaky* (see page 39), and *Forbidden Love*.

By then, some recurring patterns were well-established. The tales often use magical creatures and witchcraft, carefully researched from the old legends of Ukraine, to enchant an audience with the feel of days gone by. Other tales use picaresque adventures not only to bring different regions of Ukraine into the story, but also to create broadly comic adventures and illuminate character.

Costumes now include mysterious creations for wood nymphs and tree spirits—costumes never seen on any village square in Bukovyna or Volyn. Magic crystals sparkle; dance formations never authorized by Vasile Avramenko fill the stage.

Shumka's choreographers no longer judge authenticity by whether a dance movement is part of the original village repertoire. But a sense of cultural authenticity is still a strong cord that links the members of the troupe to their Ukrainian heritage. In the words of one long-time member, it boils down to a gut feeling that says, if ever that invisible cord is broken, "No—that just doesn't feel Ukrainian."

THREE TALES

The Calling

The Calling received its premiere in 1984 at Edmonton's Jubilee Auditorium. The story contrasts the tradition-constrained lives of Ukrainian villagers with the freedom of the spirits of the forest—and the choice that one young man has to make between two 'callings.'

As the story begins, Hutsul villagers are complaining about Vasyl, a youngster who seems to attract trouble wherever he goes. The boy is dragged into the square and berated; his awkward attempts to take part in the village dancing only manage to get him into more trouble, especially when he breaks an axe handle belonging to the biggest, strongest young man in the village.

The owner is about to expel Vasyl from the village, with the full approval of everyone, when Ivan, the elderly head shepherd, arrives. When he hears that Vasyl is a misfit and a nuisance, he offers to take him as an apprentice shepherd; perhaps that will provide an outlet for his energy and enthusiasm. Vasyl appeals to the others to let him stay. But the villagers refuse to bend. So eventually he follows Ivan, a little sad at being cast out, but also a little curious about where this new life might lead him.

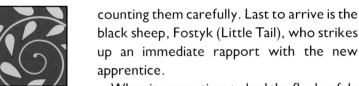

Vasyl and Ivan approach the high pasture country and the boy responds happily to the openness and freedom of the distant mountain peaks. The old man gives him a shepherd's leather vest, a bag, and a staff like his own as symbols of his new life. He also gives the boy a flute to call the flocks. Soon, there is the sound of small hooves as the sheep arrive, and Ivan shows his apprentice the basics of caring for the flock: rounding them up, herding them into a small group and, finally, counting them carefully. Last to arrive is the black sheep, Fostyk (Little Tail), who strikes up an immediate rapport with the new apprentice.

When it comes time to bed the flock safely for the night, Vasyl takes up the flute and settles down to his new responsibility of watching over the sleeping flock. Suddenly he hears his melody played back to him from the forest—but in a mocking, enticing spirit.

After a struggle against temptation, he tries to answer the call with his own flute, then dances off to find out who is calling him. In his absence, the flock wakens and wanders off. Ivan wakens and rushes off to catch the strays. As he goes, he sends the black sheep to find the foolish boy and bring him back.

Meanwhile, Vasyl has wandered deep into the forest. Villagers seldom come to places such as this; they prefer the tidy fields and open spaces of home. Suddenly, he senses he is not alone. Spirits of the forest are all around

Villagers berate Vasyl, a misfit of a boy who tries desperately to belong to the community but succeeds only in breaking buckets, axe handles, and other articles of village life.

Once Vasyl is packed off to become the apprentice to old Ivan, the shepherd, the villagers celebrate with a rousing Hutsul dance. Now that the boy is gone, the patterns of their dance can flow, uninterrupted.

Vasyl (danced by Orest Semchuk in this 1982 performance) receives the staff that represents his new life as a shepherd from Ivan (Gordon Gordey). Photo: Bill McKeown.

When the flock arrives, Vasyl learns the duties of a shepherd. The sheep are, in their own way, as cohesive a group as the villagers—except for one black sheep, Fostyk. Like Vasyl, he is always slightly out of step.

him, the mischievous ***chortyky*** who can hide in tree leaves or look like stones as they wish. The leader of the *chortyky* pulls out a flute and plays the same notes that called the boy away from his duties and responsibilities. Vasyl is once again captivated and joins in the wild dancing.

Their music brings Fostyk onto the scene. The black sheep persuades Vasyl to return to his responsibilities, although not without competition from the *chortyky*. They coax Vasyl to stay and share their unfettered life, then, in a final burst of mischief, misdirect the two travellers as they attempt to leave the forest.

Stumbling out of the woods, Vasyl and Fostyk come upon a group of Transcarpathian villagers. Always anxious to belong, the boy tries to take part, but his clumsy intrusiveness is no more successful with the Transcarpathians than with the people of his own community. The men of the village order him off. Back in the forest, the *chortyky* show up again, but Vasyl does not trust them. His mistrust is well placed, because he is promptly sent off once more in the wrong direction.

This time, the two companions emerge from the forest to find themselves at a Bukovynian picnic. The people seem prepared to welcome them into their midst, until Vasyl realizes that the black sheep has been neatly slung on a spit and is being carried off. He rushes to rescue his companion and, with the villagers in hot pursuit, they race back to the relative safety of the forest.

Once again, the *chortyky* appear. This time, Vasyl realizes that the true way home must lie in the opposite direction to the one in which they point. The forest spirits are delighted by this acumen and beg him again to stay. But the boy is determined to live up to his responsibility for getting Fostyk back to the safety of the shepherd's fold.

The scene shifts back to Vasyl's home village. Once again, Vasyl is being dragged into the square and scolded,

When Vasyl is lured away into the forest by an eerie, mocking call, he finds himself surrounded by a band of chortyky who tease and continually misdirect him. The chortyky of Ukrainian legend are mischievous, teasing spirits, neither malign nor friendly towards humans. In The Calling, *they represent the spirit world that lies beyond the neat boundaries of kitchen and farmyard. From left: John Pichlyk as the leader of the chortyky, Orest Semchuk, Luba Eshenko, Dennis Elkow, Marianna Maslo, George Chrunik, and Bill Baziuk as Fostyk.*

this time for abandoning the sheep entrusted to him. Fostyk arrives with Ivan. The old man is angry and hurt at the boy's defection, but the villagers insist that the boy is his responsibility. When he sees how thoroughly Vasyl is rejected, Ivan begins to relent. He agrees to take him back to the mountains as his apprentice if he will do as he is told and guard the sheep responsibly. The boy agrees eagerly. But just at that moment, the call is heard again—mocking, challenging. Vasyl falters and is torn; he turns to ask the shepherd what he should do.

At last, Ivan understands. He himself has heard that wild music many times. The villagers, snug in their houses, would never hear it.

"Go," he says. "That's your destiny—that's where you belong."

Vasyl removes his vest and hands it back to the old man. They embrace each other. Then Vasyl heads off to the forest, without his Hutsul jacket, and without his shepherd's vest.

The *chortyky* come out of hiding to welcome their companion—one of the rare humans who can hear their call and pass the rigorous tests of the spirit world. They leap and jump in fierce exhiliration. The void in his life filled at last, Vasyl is in perfect harmony with those around him.

ENCHANTED LOVE

Enchanted Love received its premiere on August 7, 1990 in the Taras Shevchenko Opera and Ballet Theatre, Kyiv. The story is loosely based on the play, Song of the Forest *by Lesia Ukrainka, one of Ukraine's foremost playwrights. Her play is, in turn, based on the rich folklore of her native region of Volyn. This spirit world of* **rusalky**, **mavky**, *zlydni and other spirits—both malevolent and kindly—touches every aspect of day-to-day life of human beings with its invisible fingers.*

The story opens in a clearing in the mountains of western Ukraine, as a group of young Hutsul girls comes to dance and make wreaths of braided flowers for their sweethearts. Lukash, an old man, comes into the group playing his **sopilka**. His music is fresh and youthful, compelling the girls to dance with more joy than ever.

As the girls finish their dance and depart, one of them

offers her wreath to him in a sudden impulse of gratitude. Lukash shakes his head, declining the gift. But the girl's spontaneous gesture touches a chord of memory and he pulls out a withered wreath from his pouch. It was given to him by his own love many years ago—a love who was very different from the mortal girls dancing in the meadow.

The scene shifts back fifty years or so, to another clearing in the woods. Mavka, a wood nymph, and her companions are gathering flowers for a wreath. The Hag enters. She is a mortal being who has spent the years of her long life learning spells and enchantments that give her enormous power over the mortal world, and over some aspects of the spirit world. But she remains mortal and subject to death.

At the sight of Mavka's vitality, the Hag is overcome by the desire to possess her immortality. But the mortal world and spirit cannot touch directly, and her futile attempts to touch the nymph are interrupted by sounds in the distance.

Two Hutsul men appear in the forest clearing, one of them the young Lukash. He is captivated by Mavka's beauty. Teasingly, the nymph offers him her wreath and they dance together. When Mavka is about to leave, Lukash pulls out his *sopilka* and plays a trill. The music has the same impact on her as her beauty has had on him—she is enchanted and answers his music by making the forest birds break out in an answering chorus of song.

But when the two of them reach spontaneously to embrace, they realize they cannot touch. The barrier between the mortal and spirit worlds keeps them apart; their hands pass through each other. Sobered, they stand apart and imagine what their love would be like if they could touch each other—a fantasy embodied in a *pas de deux*. As the fantasy fades, Mavka starts to leave. She offers her wreath to Lukash and turns away. He refuses to believe his fantasy cannot be made real and rushes after her.

The Hag has been watching throughout from her hiding place. She sees the attraction between the two and begins to concoct a plan to get what she wants— Mavka's youth and immortality.

The scene now shifts to preparations for the traditional mid-summer celebration. The other young men of the village arrive, carrying piles of wood for the

The mavky of Ukrainian folklore are the spirits of unbaptized children, or of children who were lost in the forest and never found. Like the water nymphs, rusalky, they are elusive creatures. They are heard in the rustle of leaves and the splash of water, but they are seldom seen by mortals. Roxanne MacLean (far right) and Teresa Manchuk (far left) dance the roles of Mavka's companion nymphs.

Cherisse Killick dances the role of Mavka, the wood nymph with whom young Lukash falls in love. In describing Mavka, Killick says, "Lukash's flute music is very like the call of the birds she lives among . . . She's free and vibrant, and yet she's willing to let go of her freedom to be with him."

The Hag, or village witch, is another familiar figure in Ukrainian folklore. She is a mortal woman who has spent years learning spells and enchantments that give her power over village life and some aspects of the immortal, spirit world. Viktor Stepovy gives the role a yearning menace in this 1990 performance. "I'm trying to steal the youth out of Mavka and put it in my own broken body."

Kathleen Todoruk and Troy Gaboury dance the fantasy love duet that expresses the longing between Lukash and Mavka. Shumka has incorporated the vocabulary of ballet to heighten choreographic moments such as this.

Lukash and Mavka discover for the first time that mortal and immortal hands cannot touch. In dancing the role of Lukash, John Zinchuk describes his character as "someone who goes after what is usually forbidden. He gets to touch a little bit of heaven but then has to come back to earth."

During a break from the confines of the rehearsal hall, Cherisse Killick and John Zinchuk go through their roles as Lukash and Mavka. They are accompanied by Valerian Markevych.

bonfire. Lukash returns and shows his wreath to his companions, but they tease him by grabbing it away and urge him to pay attention to the real world.

The exuberance of the young men breaks out in an *arkan*, and the girls enter to tease and flirt. In the middle of the dance, the sky clouds over and the dancers disperse. The Hag enters with her creatures—illusions cast to look like stacks of bonfire fuel or deadwood. She is accompanied by her apprentice, a young sorceress who wants to learn the Hag's secrets and someday possess similar powers. Lukash is surrounded by the Hag's creatures and his exit is blocked. The Hag pulls out Mavka's wreath and tells him that she can bring the two lovers together.

The scene shifts to another part of the forest. The Hag's apprentice is preparing the site for her mistress's ritual. When the Hag arrives with Lukash in tow, she begins preparing the most powerful enchantment of her long career. She calls on the older, wilder spirits of the forest to help her complete the spell. Lysovyk, king of the forest, arrives along with a covey of other spirits who cast their contributions into the brewing bowl.

The spirits leave, celebrating the power of their work. The Hag offers the potion to Lukash, refusing his offer of gold in payment and asking for his *sopilka* instead. But the young man refuses the Hag's request, grabs the potion, throws down his gold, and runs off.

The scene shifts to reveal Mavka and her companions sleeping by a clump of reeds near the river. Water nymphs emerge from their river home and dance with Mavka, until their play is interrupted by

the intrusion of the mortal world—a raft poled slowly down the river by Lukash.

The young men leap ashore and begin a rafters' dance. They are joined by girls of the village. Lukash pulls out his *sopilka* and Mavka appears, followed by her companions who join with the villagers in the dance. The Hag watches impatiently and she freezes time for a few moments to steal the *sopilka* from Lukash's belt. Then she unfreezes Lukash and Mavka and directs him to give the nymph the magic brew that will make her mortal. Against a background of frozen dancers, Mavka takes the flask.

At last, she and Lukash can touch. The Hag breaks the frozen motion of the other dancers and allows their celebration to continue. When the couples leave the clearing to head home, Lukash and his love linger behind. Then the awful reality of the Hag's spell sets in. Mavka has been made mortal, but her spirit vitality has been transferred to the malevolent being who concocted the magic brew. The Hag exults over the success of her scheme and mocks Mavka by playing a few notes on the *sopilka* that make the nymph respond feebly.

Lukash realizes there is a connection between the music and the spell and wrenches the flute back to play his own music. Slowly, it restores Mavka's vitality, and the Hag drags herself away, cheated of immortality. The lovers turn to each other overjoyed, only to realize that once again, Mavka's hands pass through Lukash's grasp. Accepting the inevitable, Mavka turns away. Lukash reaches after her, forsaken and forlorn.

Old Lukash, the *sopilka* player, reappears, holding

The design for the Hag's costume was created by Robert Shannon, based on a study of historic photographs and etchings.

Laurel Chomyc as a rusalka, *or water nymph, wakens* Mavka. *Rusalky are elusive but well-known spirits of Ukrainian folklore. During the seasons knows as Green Holydays, homes were decorated with blossoming boughs of the lime tree and no household tasks were done for fear of offending them. This sense of early summer pervades the whole story of* Enchanted Love. *Lighting Design: Witold Kurpinski.*

Mavka and her companions, the river nymphs, dance in the mist of early morning. She is unaware that Lukash is seeking her, and that a raft full of young men is being poled down the river towards this meadow. Once again, ballet and character dance set the dancing of the spirits apart from the dance of the Hutsul villagers.

Throughout Enchanted Love, *the midsummer courting rituals of the young men and women of the village form a background for the love story between Lukash and Mavka. Dancers in Hutsul dress perform a traditional dance step.*

Made mortal by the Hag's potion, Mavka can at last join the villager's dancing. She does not realize the price she must pay for this brief contact with her lover.

As Mavka's vitality fades, the Hag exults over her theft of the nymph's vitality.

the wreath that connects him now to memory and his old hopes of love. He takes out his *sopilka* and plays his music as sweetly as ever. It brings a curious sensation, as if something had brushed his cheek.

Memory? The spirit of Mavka lingering, immortal, nearby?

He does not know.

THE TRAVELLING CHUMAKY

*The **chumaky** were a common feature of Ukrainian life from the seventeenth to the mid-nineteenth century. They were wagoners and traders, whose customary route took salt and preserved fish from the Crimea-Black Sea area to trade for wheat and farm products in Poltava. The chumak profession was common among all classes, particularly among kozaks and well-to-do peasants. Their lives and customs are preserved in numerous songs and folk tales; they also inspired authors and artists.*

The Travelling Chumaky makes a rollicking, broadly comic stage performance out of one trading journey, complete with the swirling costumes and dances from various regions of Ukraine.

The story opens in the market square of a small village in the Poltava region, where three *chumaky* are preparing their two-wheeled cart before leaving on a trading journey. Hryts is the head *chumak*—gruff, business-like, and experienced. His companions are Vasyl, the ledger-keeper; and Slavko, a slightly oafish assistant.

They are attempting to repair a broken wagon wheel when Stetsko wanders by. He is an orphan, cast loose

on the world but optimistic that he will find his place. His advice on repairs is ignored, but Stetsko is unabashed. He thinks he has contributed, and a whole new world opens up for him. He will become a *chumak*!

Villagers begin to arrive in the marketplace, carrying goods that they wish the *chumaky* to carry south for trading: casks of home-brewed spirit, brightly woven cloth, and a finely made coat. Hryts checks each item and Vasyl records it in the ledger. Young men and women bring vividly coloured ribbons to be traded, and a **torban**-maker enters plucking the strings.

The scene is interrupted by the arrival of newcomers. Two gypsy women, followed by the chief of their band, have come to check out the opportunities offered on market day. In eighteenth-century Ukraine, gypsies were familiar, although they remained largely

Stetsko, a young orphan who has happened by, offers Hryts a suggestion on repairing the wagon wheel. Naive and enthusiastic, Stetsko has decided he wants to become a chumak—although his prospective colleagues are anything but encouraging.

The chumaky *prepare to go on a new trading journey. Hryts, the head* chumak, *examines merchandise brought by the people of his village, while his helper Vasyl enters items in the trading ledger.*

Young men of the traders' home village do an impromptu dance to the music of a torban *that the instrument-maker has brought to place on consignment with the* chumaky.

Stetsko (left) and Slavko struggle to help Hryts remove a too-tight pair of gypsy boots. In his first attempt at bargaining, Stetsko had traded his guard's pistol for the boots while the others slept. Unfortunately, he did not realize that, while he was making a deal with the gypsy chief, the rest of the band emptied the wagon he was supposed to guard.

The gypsy chief shares out the trade goods captured from the chumaky, over-confident that the traders will not pursue them.

The gypsies celebrate their good fortune in a wild, spirited dance, during which the women vye for attention from the men—in particular, to be the chief's choice for gypsy queen. Soon exhausted, they will sleep too soundly to realize the chumaky have crept into their camp to take back their property.

separate from the life of the towns and villages. They lived by their wits—which often meant taking advantage of the carelessness or naiveté of outsiders to relieve them of their possessions.

As trading goods continue to arrive, the chief slips around to see the merchandise being loaded into the wagon. Hryts catches him skulking around and orders him off. Finally, the wagon is full and the villagers break into a *hopak* to express their hopes of a good return from the trading venture.

As night falls, Hryts sets Slavko to guard the wagon. Slavko promptly delegates the job to the ever-eager Stetsko, offering the boy a pistol to help with the guard duties. Thrilled by this opportunity, Stetsko promises fervently to watch well. But he dozes off, giving the gypsies the opportunity they have been waiting for. Stetsko wakes up while they are unloading the cart, but the chief distracts him by offering to trade his fine leather boots for the pistol.

When the *chumaky* waken, they admire the boots. However, their good humour disappears when Hryts realizes the goods have been stolen. They rush off to get them back.

In the gypsy encampment the gypsies celebrate their success and the chief chooses one of the women as his queen. Once the revelries are over and the gypsies are sleeping, the *chumaky* slip into the camp to get their property back. The gypsies waken to find *they* have been robbed—a grave insult to their professional pride. They set off in hot pursuit of the *chumaky*. The flight lasts day after day, night after night, and the traders are nearly recaptured several times.

The scene shifts to a village in the Volyn area. The villagers' dance is interrupted by the *chumaky*, who got lost trying to elude the gypsies. Stetsko is captivated by the bright eyes of one of the village girls. Her father finds the prospect of a son-in-law in the *chumak* trade attractive but her mother is dismayed. She sabotages the betrothal negotiations by having the girl replaced by a pumpkin—the traditional symbol that a bargain has been refused. Dejected, Stetsko sets off again with his fellows.

The traders are still far from their accustomed routes. They continue to pull their wagon through unknown country while Stetsko—still clutching his pumpkin—sulks. None of them realize that the gypsies are still on their tail.

Their journeys take them to western Ukraine, where people from the mountain regions of Transcarpathia and Bukovyna have gathered for a festival. Here, Hryts takes advantage of the opportunity to trade the merchandise they have brought from Poltava. The trading goes well as the villagers offer their finest goods to the *chumaky*.

Pleased, Hryts decides it is time to set off for home. However, they are delayed by a broken wagon wheel. While they are preoccupied with repairs, the gypsies attack. Stetsko manages to escape, still carrying the wagon wheel. The gypsies force Hryts to take the part of the missing wheel as the wagon is pulled away.

The scene shifts to a *kozak* camp nearby. While the soldiers are training, they sense an intruder nearby, who turns out to be Stetsko, trundling his wagon wheel through the desolate countryside. After hearing his story, the **hetman** promptly orders his troops to remedy the situation.

Led by an enthusiastic Stetsko, the *kozaky* rush to the gypsy encampment. A grim, hand-to-hand battle betwen the *hetman* and the gypsy chief is brought to a close by a most unlikely weapon: Stetsko's pumpkin. Hryts congratulates the boy, telling him that he has now earned the right to be a *chumak*, and the traders head for home.

Arriving at their native village, they find people gathered in the market square, anxious to find out what their goods have earned. The villagers are pleased when the cart is unloaded; Hryts is pleased to have discharged his responsibilities at last; and Stetsko is pleased with his acceptance, symbolized by new *chumak* clothes. To celebrate, everyone dances a *hopak*.

Hryts asks for directions from the people of a Volyn village. The chumaky *are far from their accustomed trading routes at this point, having become lost as they tried to elude the vengeful gypsies. Stetsko falls in love with a Volynian sweetheart only to have his suit rejected by the girl's mother.*

Stetsko wanders into another village, still holding the pumpkin that is the token of his rejected suit in Volyn. The chumaky *now find themselves in the middle of a festival where people have gathered from the mountain regions of Transcarpathia and Bukovyna. Even though the* chumaky *are still far from their accustomed trading areas, Hryts will finally have the opportunity to exchange his goods profitably so that the traders can start home.*

Kozaky show off their agility and strength, unaware that only a short distance away, Hryts and his companions have finally been captured by the gypsy band. However, Stetsko has been able to escape and finds his way to the kozak camp.

A grim, hand-to-hand battle between the kozak leader and the gypsy chief is brought to an end with an unexpected weapon —Stetsko's pumpkin.

After the chumaky have returned home, Stetsko helps distribute the merchandise acquired on their journey.

PROFILE:
Orest Semchuk

With Orest Semchuk as artistic director, Shumka crossed the subtle line that divides folk art from theatre. Chester Kuc had been conscious of the need to entertain audiences and improve technique. But Orest wanted to involve audiences in a new way. He wanted them to respond not only because they felt attached to the Ukrainian heritage being presented on stage, but also because they were moved by the emotions portrayed.

He retained the deep respect for authenticity established as a groundwork by Kuc. But he felt that Ukrainian dance could be freshened and enhanced, and that he could legitimately move outside the Ukrainian community for professional theatre help.

"We weren't awestruck about dance as a sort of untouchable traditional and aesthetic icon," he says. "To us, it always had to be entertaining."

During an interview in the early 1970s, he described his approach to choreography. "It modernizes the display only, but doesn't change the tradition."

The change to a more theatrical focus was a process of evolution, not unlike the one by which Orest himself grew into the position of artistic director. In 1961, at the age of fourteen, he began dancing with the group; by the age of seventeen, he was choreographing dances and leading warm-up sessions, working more and more closely with Kuc.

There never was a formal job interview or newspaper announcement, but by the late 1960s, Semchuk was juggling sociology classes at the University of

Orest Semchuk was artistic director of Shumka throughout the 1970s and early 1980s. He set new standards for artistic collaboration and teamwork, both onstage and off.

Two Shumka dancers-to-be: Orest Semchuk and Khrystyna Yopuk, circa 1954.

Alberta with the responsibility of being Shumka's artistic director. He was a skinny 21-year-old with the longish hair of the decade and a high energy level—a scavenger of ideas, a builder of visions.

Kuc's decision to leave Shumka reflected some bitterness and cleavages within the group. The very calibre of the dancers he had recruited ensured that people had minds and creative wills of their own that sometimes came into conflict with the founding director's compelling vision of Shumka.

As his successor, Semchuk undertook to heal this bitterness. Methodical and demanding, he was nevertheless approachable and open to suggestions from any member of the troupe. He established a choreographic committee, allowing any dancer to try his or her choreographic talents. This open approach posed its risks, but Orest and other experienced members of the company were always there as a safety net.

"He had a consistency about him that was both inspirational and soothing," recalls one dancer.

Semchuk's successor as artistic director, John Pichlyk, recalls him as "a very quiet man. . . . The secret to his success was simply that he was very patient. If he couldn't get something out of the dancers in one way, he would evaluate his strategy and come in through the back door and get it another way."

Rehearsals were demanding but on the whole relaxed and enjoyable. Semchuk had an unassuming appearance compared with Kuc's tall figure, recalls Gordon Gordey. He remembers him leading rehearsals in blue jeans with rolled-up cuffs, a white T-shirt, and white girls' sneakers "because their soles allowed the best extension."

"Simplicity is beauty," was one of Orest's favourite axioms. He insisted on clean technique and precision in steps and demanded that the corps perform as a disciplined whole. Before a major show, he would have the dancers meet on the stage and give them a word or phrase such as "togetherness" on which to concentrate.

Under his directorship, story-lines really began to develop. (See page 18.) He strove for clarity in the telling of tales.

"Story-lines have to be clearly expressed so the audience never has to refer to a program to find out what is going on. To my mind, dance should not have a secret language."

The second major thrust of Semchuk's directorship was the development and polishing of the dancers themselves. Trained in ballet, he looked to ballet, jazz, and other ethnic dance traditions for ideas and techniques. He pulled in a long line of workshops and guest teachers during the 1970s to pass these skills on to his group.

The lessons were obviously well learned. Semchuk had to explain countless times that, no, Shumka is not made up of professional dancers. People found it hard to believe that amateurs could aspire to and achieve such professional standards.

The answer, he feels, may have something to do with the freedom an amateur status creates.

"It could be that, when you pour your heart and soul into something you love and you don't have to do it for a living, you do it better."

Orest Semchuk with a group of dancers who played key roles in the development of Shumka after Chester Kuc's departure as artistic director. Males, clockwise from far left: Gene Zwozdesky, Levern Wasylynchuk, Vlad Eshenko, Orest Semchuk, Oleh Lukomskyj, Richard Scherban. Females, from left: Elaine Dasko, Mary Kolynsky, Marion Ostapchuk, Audrey Morello, Betty Faryna, Dianne Ross (centre).

Like all Shumka's artistic directors and choreographers, Orest Semchuk was also a dancer. Here, he flies through the air as part of a flirtation dance performed in 1969. Photo: Walter Bartko.

PART 3

DEVELOPING STAGECRAFT

"There is no doubt the Shumka Dancers are making a marked contribution to the preservation of Canada's rich Ukrainian heritage. It is always gratifying to pay tribute to genuine talent."

—Stanley Bligh, Vancouver Sun, 1964

DANCE AND COSTUME:
The Regions of Ukraine

INTRODUCTION

SHUMKA'S AUDIENCES SEE masses of colour, intricate shapes painted by lines of dancers, sudden jabs of vibrant colour and motion. They see excitement, grace, energy.

The palette of colours, textures, movements with which these pictures are created is not selected arbitrarily by artistic directors or choreographers. Instead, it is a palette that has been developed and handed down through centuries. It is an aesthetic whole that defines the Ukrainian people, stitch by stitch of embroidered wool, step by step of a circle dance.

*Roxanne MacLean wears the costume of a nineteenth-century young woman of Poltava. Her **vinok** is the headwear for which girls have gathered flowers from time immemorial.*

Ethnographic Regions of Ukraine – Late 19th Century

POLAND

Lemkivshchyna

CZECHOSLOVAKIA

HUNGARY

BYELORUSSIA

RUSSIA

POLISSIA

• Lviv

VOLYN

HALYCHYNA

Boikivshchyna

Kyiv •

Dnipro River

TRANSCARPATHIA

BUKOVYNA

PODILLIA

Central
Ukraine

• Poltava

Hutsulshchyna

ROMANIA

Southern
Ukraine

KUBAN

Sea of Azov

Black Sea

CRIMEA

— **Ethnographic boundaries**
— **Ethnolinguistic boundary**
— **Political boundaries**

The ethonographic regions of Ukraine are not rigidly marked; instead, differences in folk dance and folk dress tend to shade into one another, making a rich tapestry of styles and variations on certain common themes. In general, the people of the western mountainous regions have been more isolated. As a result, their dance and dress retain features that are more clearly defined than those of the central Ukrainian plain.

It is also an aesthetic whole that defines Shumka performances. Authenticity—the colours used on a jacket, the cut of a dancer's shirt—is a matter for scrupulous attention.

Fortunately for stage designers, the palette they work with is exceptionally rich and varied. The dances and dress of Ukraine share certain basic patterns; but they differ subtly from region to region, district to district, village to village.

To make the costumes for a Shumka production takes 2100 m of fabric and more than 43 000 m of embroidery thread.

THE BASICS OF FOLK DRESS

The basic Ukrainian garments evolved over many generations: the **sorochka**, a shirt of white homespun cloth, worn by both men and women; pants for men and wrap-around skirts for women; sashes; and sleeveless jackets known as **korsetky** or **keptari**. These basic garments were adapted to the needs and aesthetic tastes within a region, district, or village.

Headwear identified the marital status of a woman. Unmarried girls often wore the well-known *vinok*, or wreath, while married women throughout Ukraine wore their hair covered in public. Folk ceremonies involved covering a bride's head to symbolize the transition to married life.

Colours of clothing were generally bright and clear. In many regions, primary colours predominated, although pastel shades were characteristic of Poltava. Embroidery was an almost universal method of decoration, and on festive garments it became very elaborate.

For the ancient Slavic tribes, certain geometric patterns had a talismanic significance. They were embroidered at the openings of the sleeves, neck, and hem of a garment for protection against evil spirits. The clothing worn by young women was more highly decorated because of their greater vulnerability during childbirth. This talismanic tradition evolved into numerous superstitions around the making of clothing. For instance, Thursday was felt to be the best day to begin sewing a shirt. Embroidery with many knots was held to ensure a long life for the wearer.

Later, embroidery became an expression of the creativity and identity with a given social group. The original repertoire of geometric patterns was expanded to include floral and other motifs.

In adapting folk dress for the stage, Shumka generally draws on costumes representing the Sunday best of various regions, as worn in the eighteenth and nineteenth centuries. To some extent, this adaptation represents a necessary simplification of the rich variety of folk dress within each region. In its early years, the company drew primarily on the Hutsul and Poltava regions. Over the past fifteen years, the dedicated involvement and research of individuals like Elsie Chanasyk have broadened Shumka's repertoire of stage costume to represent other regions of Ukraine.

THE BASICS OF FOLK DANCE

The majority of Ukrainian folk dances evolved from ancient circle dances, which developed over the centuries into pair and couple dances. Today, the original circle dances are enriched by many intricate figures. Dancers tend to move in linear or geometrical patterns—circle, cross, serpent, chain—forming rounded lines. Generally, these patterns unfold in a horizontal direction, although dances of the mountain regions feature vertical leaps and lifts.

These circular dances contain many ancient elements, with traditional steps directly linked to pre-Christian ritual dances. Some steps reflect an imitation of working movements: stamping in seeds at planting, weaving, or digging into the soil.

Another major category of Ukrainian folk dance is the topical dance, which includes dances reflecting social customs, events from everyday life, and humourous dances based on the behaviour of beasts or birds. Most of these dances are performed to music in 2/4 time, based on one or two steps, and diverse in composition.

Even though there are common elements shared by all regions of Ukraine, dances differ strongly from one area to the next in their choreographic methods, content, and dynamics.

One important shared feature is the role of female dancers. They dance with great agility and rhythm, flirt

This engraving of nineteenth century folk costume in Bukovyna shows, from left: a Hutsul couple, a Ukrainian woman, and a Romanian man.

Shumka members gather at the Museum of Folk Architecture and Folk Life in Lviv, wearing the costumes of Transcarpathia (left), Hutsul region (right), and Poltava (centre). For its stage interpretation of dress and dance, Shumka chooses typical characteristics of the various regions based on careful research. This represents a necessary simplification of the many variations found within each region. Ukraine Photos: Gordon Gordey.

with their partners, but always move with dignity and grace.

CENTRAL UKRAINE

OVERVIEW

Black *chernozem* topsoil is a metre deep. Slow, side-winding rivers. Fertility as far as the eye can see.

The broad fields of central Ukraine are generous producers of grain, making it no surprise that Ukrainian people sometimes call themselves **khliboroby**.

Poltava is one of the ancient cities of east-central Ukraine. It is especially significant to the Ukrainian sense of national identity because the Ukrainian language and literature were first revived there after almost complete extinction at the end of the eighteenth century.

The stage dress that one thinks of as typically Ukrainian—red boots and wide pantaloons for a man, wreaths of flowers and ribbons in a girls' hair—represents the folk dress of the Poltava district. Ukraine's national instrument, the **bandura** also comes from this part of the country.

FOLK DRESS

Voluminous sleeves gathered tight at the cuff and equally voluminous **sharavary** tucked into their boots give men from Poltava a distinctive, dashing silhouette in Shumka's stage performances. This costume calls for a lot of fabric. As one old saying goes, *sharavary* should be "as wide as the Black Sea," and the **poias** was "ten to twelve elbows long" and wrapped several times around the waist.

In summer weather, many men wear a *bryl*, a shallow-crowned, wide-brimmed hat woven from rye or wheat straw. The *shapka* is a tall, cylindrical hat of gray or black lambskin for colder weather.

A Poltava woman's sleeves are also wide and flowing, with a wide band embroidered below the shoulder. Embroidery is typically stitched in red and black floral designs. Her trim skirt is made of a doubled length of cloth wrapped around the waist. It is short enough to reveal the embroidered hem of her *sorochka* below and her festive boots of soft red leather.

Over the skirt she wears a **fartukh** decorated with woven designs or strips of embroidery. She also wears

a *korsetka*. Sometimes this is neatly fitted to the waist, while in other parts of central Ukraine it is cut more squarely.

One of the most characteristic features of an unmarried girl's costume is the *vinok*, lovingly braided with poppy flowers, blue cornflowers, white camomile and wild roses and set on top of a flutter of ribbons.

DANCES

The dances of the Poltava differ from dances of the western, mountainous regions in that dancers do not always move in geometric formations like lines or circles. Instead, men and women often move individually, the dance style allowing great freedom of expression and improvisation.

Poltava dancers move in broad, smooth curves. Often the music starts slowly, then accelerates while the women tap an infinite variety of rhythms with the metal *pidkivky* on their boots. Meanwhile, the men's heels fly in **prysiadky**, that outward thrust with the foot delivered from a squatting position. It's an athletic feat requiring Olympic-level endurance.

This is the country where the *hopak* originated, one of the most familiar Ukrainian dance traditions to North American audiences. *Hopak*, which derives its name from the word for "jump," was originally a men's dance. It evolved into a mixed dance, although the men's acrobatic solos retain a prominent role.

The *hopak* is joyous, exuberant, and improvisational in nature. Individual dancers select steps and invent combinations freely; no two dancers necessarily do the same step at the same time. Partners keep an eye on each other, smiling and flirting as they move.

Another popular dance of central Ukraine is the **kozachok**, which evolved from the *hopak* as far back as the sixteenth century. The main difference is that women take on a central role in the *kozachok*. Instead of beginning slowly and accelerating, music for the *kozachok* is faster and lighter throughout. This showcases the women, allowing them to stamp out many different, intricate steps at blistering speed.

Dancers wear Shumka's stage version of Poltava folk dress, photographed at the Museum of Folk Life and Folk Architecture in Kyiv. The folk dress of this region in central Ukraine is the most familiar to North Americans and most likely to be thought of as typically Ukrainian.

The wide sharavary worn by men of central Ukraine are well adapted for riding horseback, or for performing the flying leaps of the hopak. Hopak originated as a dance for males only, and to this day the men's acrobatic solos are a prominent feature.

HUTSUL

OVERVIEW

The Hutsul region is a small area on the highest slopes of the Carpathian Mountains. The Hutsul people were primarily shepherds and woodsmen, who coaxed crops out of harsh mountainsides.

The isolation of this rugged terrain has preserved the past vividly. Many Hutsul folk customs and beliefs go back to archaic ways of life and pre-Christian elements.

FOLK DRESS

The folk dress of the Hutsul people uses less cloth than that worn in central Ukraine, and the overall silhouette is not so loose and voluminous.

Sleeves of the *sorochka* are narrower. Men's shirts are finished with a low stand-up collar instead of the

circular hole used in Poltava. Men's **shtany** are relatively slim, made without folds and gathers. As well as the normal woven sash, Hutsul men wear the *cheres*. It is a leather belt about 40 cm wide and helps support the back and stomach muscles in heavy work.

A Hutsul woman's skirt consists of two separate rectangles of fabric tied around the waist. The resulting split at either side makes a practical garment for riding. The colour varies from area to area: bright yellow in Kosmach, light brown in Verkhovyna.

In the Hutsul region, the vest takes the form of the *keptar*. This is shorter and squarer than the *korsetka* worn in Poltava, and is worn by both men and women. The vest is made of sheepskin, distinctively and elaborately decorated with Morroccan leather, metal studs, and woolen embroidery.

Embroidery of the Hutsul region is typically stitched in geometrical shapes of triangles and diamonds. These

Shumka members wearing the costume of the mountainous Hutsul region, photographed near Jasper, Alberta.

These characteristic items of Hutsul dress were made in the 1800s. The keptar is made of sheepskin and elaborately decorated; the fine boots have horseshoe-shaped metal plates on each heel to help their wearer walk the mountain slopes.

The **trembita,** *shown in this picture of a Hutsul family in the nineteenth century, was a horn used primarily to signal events like the arrival of visitors or enemies. Most often made of spruce split in half, hollowed, then glued together, its call could be heard clearly from mountain peak to mountain peak.*

Shumka dancers wear their Hutsul costume, photographed at Lviv's Museum of Folk Architecture and Folk Life. The women wear the uplitka, *headwear made of braided red wool. The elaborate embroidery would be typical of Sunday best worn in the nineteenth century.*

Hutsul dances are most often circular in form—an ancient form that reflects the unity of the village. Here, Annette Bidniak and her companions are carried by the strong clasp of the male dancers in a traditional movement from a kolomyika.

are another indication of the pre-Christian roots of Ukrainian culture, representing ancient patterns that once had magical significance. Patterns based on flowers and leaves were rare in this part of Ukraine.

Another survival of the ancient times is the *uplitka*. It is made of braided red wool and wrapped around the head. In former times, it may have been woven into a braid of hair.

Old forms of footwear are also found here, such as the *lychaky*. These are woven from fibrous inner bark of trees such as the linden and are simply tied onto the foot with string. From this evolved the *postoly* worn in many regions of Ukraine. They are leather, slipper-like shoes which are tied or buckled onto the foot.

DANCE

Traditional Hutsul dance traditions are fast, fiery, and spirited. They have a strong vertical thrust featuring high leaps; women are lifted from the ground by their partners.

Most Hutsul dances are based on a circular formation—an ancient form that possibly symbolizes ancient, sun-worshipping rituals. Guests at any Ukrainian wedding in western Canada will leap up at the sounds of the *kolomyika*, traced back at least as far as the sixteenth century. It is based on the circular Hutsul tradition that today symbolizes the bonds linking lovers and friends in a new country. Dancers clasp each other by the hands or the shoulders, or join in a *hrebinka*, in which alternate dancers take hands behind their neighbour's back.

Other well-known dances associated with the Hutsul region are the *arkan* and the *hutsulka*, which became very popular in the nineteenth century. The latter dance reflects the influence of increasing contact between this region and other parts of Ukraine. It is a hybrid between the central Ukrainian *kozachok* and the *kolomyika*.

TRANSCARPATHIA

OVERVIEW

Transcarpathia lies tucked along the crescent of the Carpathians, separated from the rest of Ukraine to the east by the high spine of the mountains. The protective mountains block cold air from the north. Orchards and vineyards flourish in a landscape of valleys, streams, and sloping hills.

To the southwest, Transcarpathia descends into a fertile lowland that lies towards the present-day Hungarian border, opening up this region to influences from Hungarian and Slovakian neighbours. People live primarily in the lowlands, going up into the mountains in summer to pasture their sheep and cattle.

FOLK DRESS

Transcarpathian folk dress has a decided flavour of Hungarian and Central European dress. This is partly due to the wide, fully gathered skirts worn by women and the style and placement of embroidery patterns. *Sorochky* are distinguished by the smocking that creates rows of tiny tucks on the shirt front and by the frilled cuff.

Women's costumes are finished with an apron sometimes as big as the skirt it covers, an embroidered bolero-type vest, and a floral kerchief.

For men, the *sorochka* is shorter than in other regions of Ukraine. In fact, it sometimes ends just below the breastbone, although it is cut longer at the back. The pants worn with this style of shirt are wide-legged and end above the ankle, reminiscent of the trousers worn by gauchos of South America.

In higher regions, the folk dress more closely resembled Hutsul dress.

DANCE

Transcarpathian dances blend the Hutsul culture of the mountains with Hungarian dances like the *czardas*. Many are localized and danced only in a small region, like the *rakhivchanka*, named for the area around the city of Rakhiv in eastern Transcarpathia.

In general, the dances are fast and involve very small, rhythmic steps. The steps are quick, often in quadruple time, and are performed flatfooted. The dancer's whole body seems to vibrate.

As in neighbouring mountain areas, dances are often performed in circles and in couples. However, the Hungarian influence is seen in a great deal of improvisation. Men spin and twirl their partners, whose wide

The influence of nearby Hungary is felt in Transcarpathia, both in dance movements such as this, and in elements of folk dress.

Shumka dancers wear bright costumes representing Transcarpathian folk dress. Women of this region wear gathered skirts and colourful aprons and men wear wide-legged pants.

skirts flash from behind coloured aprons.

The *czardas* appears in many variants, both Ukrainian and Hungarian. It is primarily a couple's dance, often with a slow section followed by a faster, spinning part.

BUKOVYNA

OVERVIEW

The ethnographic region of Bukovyna merges with the Hutsul region on the eastern flank of the Carpathian Mountains. It straddles the present border between Ukraine and Romania. It is a land of varied terrain, including mountains, foothills, and the flat plain crossed by the Prut River.

FOLK DRESS

Shumka's Bukovynian stage costume has a slender, elegant appearance, accentuated by the slim skirts and high head-dresses of the women. The legs of the men's *shtany* are narrow and longer than worn in other regions of Ukraine.

The *horbotka* worn by many Bukovynian women is a distinctive garment. It is made from a rectangular piece of woven wool wrapped around the waist and fastened in front. One corner of the fabric is tucked up into the waist to provide greater freedom of movement, creating a graceful diagonal line with the ankle-length *sorochky* peeping below.

Men and women of Bukovyna wear a *keptar*. It is made of sheep or lambskin tanned almost to white and decorated along the edges with pieces of coloured leather, coloured cloth, or fur.

DANCE

Bukovynians share many dance traditions with their Hutsul neighbours. The *kolomyika* is particularly popular, with almost as many variations as there are villages in the region.

The *kolomyika's* original circle formation evolved into many versions, partly because of the influence of mixed-couple dances from other areas. Sometimes larger circles break into small ones, down to a single pair of dancers.

The variations on the circle pattern are numerous. Sometimes dancers in relatively small circles spin as fast as they can, lifting the women's feet off the floor. In other formations, men clasp hands, forming cradles where the women sit. Often, dancers or bystanders accompany *kolomyika* melodies with songs of short verses with jokes or images of everyday life.

In Bukovyna, traditional Ukrainian dances are salted with Romanian forms like the **hora**. Typically, the *hora* is performed in a closed circle. Steps are generally moderately paced and quite simple so that all the villagers, young and old, can participate. Dancers keep their elbows bent and hands held almost at shoulder height, so that the arms of adjacent dancers form a characteristic "W" shape. Numerous variants of the *hora* developed in northern Bukovyna now rank clearly as part of the Ukrainian culture.

VOLYN

OVERVIEW

Volyn stretches from the foothills of the Podolian plain northwest to the swamplands of Polissia, on the northwest border of Ukraine. Southern Volyn is a fertile area where grain waves in the fields. Here, traditions and legends linger that are as ancient as those of the Hutsul region.

FOLK DANCE

The pre-twentieth-century folk dress of Volyn differed only subtly from that of Polissia to the north. When Shumka's audiences see Volyn costumes on stage, they are likely to be reminded of folk dress in other parts of Central Europe. This is partly due to the women's skirts, which are wide and gathered to the waist, swinging like big bells in the dance. Women also typically wear a *bezrukavka*, a vest with a deeply scooped neckline. It fits closely to the waist, then flares into a short, scalloped peplum.

Their *sorochky* of white linen are almost always embroidered in red, making cuff-like swathes of colour around the lower sleeve. The upper sleeve is gathered, as are the cuffs. Women wear bright, close-fitting headpieces or white caps with kerchiefs wrapped around them.

Men of Volyn wear the straight-legged *shtany* typical of the mountains rather than the baggy *sharavary* of the central plains. The embroidery on their shirts

Shumka dancers dressed in Bukovynian costume perform a circle dance at Lviv's Museum of Folk Architecture and Folk Life. The distinctive diagonal line of the women's skirts is created by tucking a corner of the hem into the waistband.

Shumka's depiction of Bukovynian dress shows one of the styles of keptari *and* shtany *worn by men of the region.*

The whirling couple dances of Volyn emphasize the long-skirted coats of men and the full, gathered skirts worn by women.

Shumka's interpretation of Volynian dress shows the typical red embroidery on the sleeves of a women's sorochka, *and the horizontal stripes of her apron. Volynian folk dress is generally very similar to that of Polissia to the north.*

makes relatively narrow strips around collar and cuffs. Both men and women wear *svyty*, knee-length outer coats of grey cloth.

DANCE

The long rule by Poland is reflected in the dance traditions of Volyn. The *polka, mazurka, krakowiak* and other whirling couple dances have been popular for generations. The hopping, spinning movements are emphasized by the swish of the women's skirts and the long grey jackets of the men.

KOZAKY

OVERVIEW

The term *kozaky* did not at first define people of a specific ethnographic origin. Rather, it applied to a social class.

The word derives from the Turkic *kazak*, meaning "free man." It came into use in Ukraine during the sixteenth century to describe "free men" who fled beyond the feudal authorities to live in frontier territory claimed by no one. Any Christian male was free to join the *kozak* brotherhood, while women and children were barred from entry.

Two groups evolved. The Zaporizhzhian *kozaky* were named for the area of the southern steppes in which they lived. The area, Za porohamy, lay south of the rapids created as the Dnipro River dropped from the central Ukraine plateau to the Black Sea lowlands.

The *kozaky* built settlements known as **sichy** on islands in the river, which served as military camps. The Zaporizhzhian *kozaky* numbered between 5000 and 6000, although only about ten per cent of this number might be in the garrisons at any one time. The rest would return to their civilian lives and families.

Zaporizhzhia lay beyond the effective reach of Polish-Lithuanian authority, and the *kozaky* became known as freedom fighters in the seventeenth century for their struggles against this authority. Their efforts led to the creation of a *kozak* state that lasted until Empress Catherine II destroyed Nova Sich, the military centre of Zaporizhzhia, in 1775.

The second group, "Town Cossacks," lived in and around frontier communities, where they served as a border militia. They were sanctioned by the Polish-Lithuanian authorities and inscribed in a register that numbered nearly 3000 by 1589.

FOLK DRESS

Kozaky wore the wide, baggy *sharavary* of central Ukraine, a garment well adapted to horsemanship. Over their shirts, they wore a **zhupan**. This was a long-sleeved, knee-length garment of taffeta or broadcloth. The *zhupan* had a fitted waist and was sometimes made with a pleat at the back. It was often belted with a sash and sported gold or silver buttons.

Standard parts of the *kozak's* gear were his sword, pistol, and powder horn—the weapons with which he carried out his military tasks.

DANCE

The *kozak's* legacy to Ukrainian dance is the *hopak*, originally developed as a men-only dance in the island camps. It expressed the rugged, boisterous life of the *kozak*, as solo dancers improvised exuberantly on a variety of steps.

Many of these steps are said to have developed from the actions typical of *kozak* life. For instance, the *prysiadky* suggest the rhythm of riding horseback. Other steps are said to have evolved from leaping high like a falcon attacking prey or standing up in the stirrups.

Povzunets, is a low-to-the-ground step with movements that supposedly reflected crouching and stalking through the tall steppe grasses.

All these movements require strength and agility, providing an ideal showcase for male prowess.

It takes 94 sq. m of leather to make the footwear for a Shumka production.

DEVELOPMENT OF DANCE TECHNIQUE

While Shumka's choreography had developed continuously under the pull of story-lines, the company's dance technique had also undergone substantial development since the early days. Skills and approaches

The military, masculine life of the kozaky is shown clearly in Shumka's staging of kozak dances and story-line episodes using kozak characters. Kozaky wore the wide, pantaloon-like sharavary of central Ukraine.

from other dance forms were incorporated into the Ukrainian dance base.

Ballet was one of the earliest influences to be felt, introduced by Orest Semchuk, even before he became artistic director. He had studied ballet with Edmonton teacher Edith Heavener, and over the years learned to appreciate the 'why' of classical positions and how they created strong, aesthetically pleasing lines.

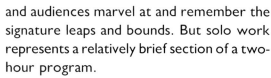

The simple raised arms of traditional dance became arms raised in the fourth position. Applied to Ukrainian dance, the ballet positions gave precision and elegance to the overall ensemble, and gave power and presentation to individuals.

But ballet was only a beginning. During the 1970s, Shumka brought in modern-dance choreographer Brian Foley, who choreographed for ice-skater Toller Cranston, to teach new ways of lifting a partner. Experts came to show them how to make sword combat believable on stage.

Taras Semchuk, brother of Orest and a dancer with the Ballet Rambert in England, taught workshops in ballet. In 1975, Shumka brought from New York Roma Pryma-Bohachevsky, a vibrant, energetic teacher of ballet and Ukrainian dance, who was a major influence on John Pichlyk.

The trend to specialized workshops continued into the 1980s. For instance, Viktor Stepovy joined the company after growing up in Ukraine and attending the famous Virsky dance school in Kyiv. He became a resource for regional choreography, broadening the company's repertoire beyond its original roots in Hutsul and Poltava dance.

This enrichment of Shumka's technical skills was reinforced by awarding scholarships that allowed dancers to study or attend workshops and bring new ideas back to the company. Shumka formalized this approach in 1974 by establishing an annual scholarship, although it began in the late 1960s. One of the original recipients was Joe Stanishewsky, who was granted a sum to enable him to study with the Alberta Ballet School. One of several Shumka dancers who have made careers in non-Ukrainian dance, Stanishewsky later went on to dance with Les Feux Follets.

One important aspect of dance technique involves the relationship between the soloists and the corps dancers. Solo work is often the focus of rehearsals, and audiences marvel at and remember the signature leaps and bounds. But solo work represents a relatively brief section of a two-hour program.

"All dancers have to be corps dancers—that means the soloists as well. All equal. All important," maintained Semchuk, who worked hard to imbue the company with this ensemble philosophy.

A related development took place in the relationship between male and female dancers. In the early days there was a tendency to use female dancers as a kind of background decoration for the acrobatic solos of the men.

"The complaint was that the girls never did anything. They were background, while the boys stole the show," recalls Chester Kuc.

Natalka Dobrolige did much to resist this tendency in the early years of the company. Semchuk recalls that she was a creative choreographer who would "try and pull away from the four-corner dance thing," established by Avramenko's training. In the process, she put her trademark stamp on the girls' dancing.

"She made the women so elegant, so strong," says John Pichlyk, who experienced her work later while she was instructing for the Vesnianka dancers in Thunder Bay.

Dobrolige and Lecia Polujan, who also choreographed many early dances, set a high standard for female dancers. Subsequently, their approach was incorporated by Semchuk into his own philosophy. His emphasis on precision also helped women take their place in the forefront.

The development of story-lines with strong female characters and the incorporation of other dance traditions, such as gypsy dance, have provided legitimate ways to open up choreography for female dancers.

The changes in dance technique over the years have been remarkable. Today, the technical requirements for a dancer coming into Shumka are much higher.

"It used to be that if you could do *prysiadky* for five minutes straight, you were automatically in," recalls Pichlyk. "Now the question is, 'What else have you got?'" New members of the company bring ten to fifteen years of dance training, not only in Ukrainian dance, but also in disciplines like ballet, jazz, and modern dance.

Over the years, Shumka has deliberately worked to acquire the techniques of ballet and other dance forms to enhance the presentation of traditional Ukrainian movements. The elegance of dancers like Terry Mucha demonstrate the impact of this development on a step from hopak.

A corps of dancers working as one became a hallmark of Shumka's style, particularly under the guidance of Orest Semchuk as artistic director. All members of the company take part in the corps—even soloists.

Over the years, female dancers have emerged from the background to play their own role in creating emotion on stage. The tradition had been to use women primarily as a backdrop for the energetic solos of male dancers, but that tradition began to be challenged shortly after Shumka's founding. Here, Hulyna Elkow creates a dramatic moment during a performance in 1979. Photo: Con Boland.

Orest Fialka expresses vitality throughout his whole body as he executes a prysiadka. The step, which calls for this kind of exuberance in a hopak, may express a very different emotion during the opening welcome dance. Dancers must use all their physical and emotional skills to convey exactly the right idea to the audience.

The other major change is the need to communicate emotions. Gone are the days when dancers were instructed to keep smiling at all times.

As Pichlyk says, "Each choreographic movement must be inspired by an understanding or interpretation of an emotion . . . the *prysiadka* step done as part of the welcome dance is different from the same step done as part of a *hopak* dance. Our task as serious dancers is to communicate the subtle difference between them."

DEVELOPMENT OF MUSIC

Music is as closely interwoven with Shumka's development as the sound of a *bandura* is with life in a Ukrainian village. So it is appropriate that the group's name derives from a piece of music.

A handwritten copy of a dance number called *Ukrainian Shumka* had been presented to Luba Stangret by Professor Barbaruk, who toured Alberta with his family in 1955 entertaining audiences with renditions of Ukrainian ballads. Over post-rehearsal coffee in the Casino Cafe one evening, Stangret suggested the word as a possible name for their new group. The word *shumka* refers to a specific traditional happy dance. However, for members of the company it took on the additional meaning of "whirlwind"—to the point where it is often assumed that this is the original translation.

Eighteenth-century bandura.

Today, the musical and visual aspects of performance are closely interwoven.

"I have always believed that fifty per cent of what you see is what you hear," says Gene Zwozdesky, the company's music director since the early 1970s.

THE ROOTS OF UKRAINIAN MUSIC

Hutsul dance traditions preserve one of the oldest accompaniments to dance: the human voice. The sweet and mournful or cheerfully rhythmic melodies preserved in the western mountains go back centuries. In preserving the traditional songs, the Ukrainian people have also preserved the language in which they are sung, and the customs and legends about which they were composed.

The instruments that give Ukrainian music its distinctive sound also have a long history. An eleventh-century fresco in the church of St. Sophia in Kyiv shows that instrumental music was already well established. Musicians are pictured playing wind instruments such as the *sopilka*; stringed instruments, including a **husli**; a bandura-like instrument; and cymbals.

Documents from the seventeenth century indicate that rural Ukrainians played violins, the **kobza**, pipes, and bagpipes in the north. Town dwellers added the *tsymbaly*, lute, and *bandura*.

By the nineteenth century, the **troisti muzyky** had stabilized as a standard accompaniment to folk dances. These included the violin and a percussion or bass instrument. The third instrument varied and could include a *tsymbaly* or a **basolia**.

Traditional instruments that create a distinctive Ukrainian sound came to Canada with early immigrants. This 1930s photograph of the Petryshyn Orchestra near Swan Plain, Saskatchewan shows a typical combination. From left: basolia, violins, and tsymbaly.

SHUMKA'S MUSICAL DEVELOPMENT

As Shumka's founding director, Chester Kuc established a tradition of accompanying dance with live music that has been a contant throughout the company's history. In the early days, the sound of Chester Kuc at the piano accompanied by his wife Luba on the violin was a common one in rehearsals and performances.

A key figure in the group's musical development is Walter Chornowol. Chornowol was born in Ukraine and studied violin from the age of ten. After emigrating to Canada in 1949, he became a member of the Edmonton Symphony Orchestra and also conducted a small dance orchestra of his own. He conducted Shumka's first concert in 1959, and worked regularly with Shumka throughout its first decade.

In the early days little musical material was available from Ukraine. Dances came primarily from the Hutsul and Poltava regions and research about the music of other regions was scarce. To compensate, arrangers such as Serge Eremenko worked hard to transcribe Ukrainian melodies from Soviet recordings.

A typical orchestra at a Shumka concert in the mid-1960s consisted of about eleven musicians: four violins, a double bass, flute, clarinet, bassoon, accordion, piano and percussion.

As story-lines developed in complexity and plot, music evolved with them. The requirements of a story-line lasting forty or fifty minutes required much more than the eight to twelve bars of melody used by the old Avramenko repertoire. Variation was required to keep audiences interested, to create mood, and to outline character. For a typical Shumka show today, music director Gene Zwozdesky provides more than 300 distinctive tempos.

In Zwozdesky's words, Shumka's music has become

Sharon Beckstead, Shumka's music librarian since the mid-1970s, organizes professional music copyists who spend approximately 800 hours preparing the orchestral scores for a typical performance.

a way of painting a choreographic moment and intensifying the audience's experience. To achieve this goal, he takes original Ukrainian melodies or composes new ones, working with musicians such as Teddy Borowiecki and Valerian Markevych. He will also go beyond the strict lexicon of Ukrainian music to use other traditions, such as gypsy or Georgian music, if they are needed for a story-line.

This type of musical borrowing "demonstrates an openess," he says. "We can go beyond our culture and bring new things back into it."

After arranging the musical sequence required by the choreography, he works out the orchestration, outlining which instrument plays what part. This has become a much more demanding task than it was when Shumka was accompanied by a dozen musicians.

On the Ukraine tour, for instance, the orchestra consisted of approximately thirty-five people, including the Kyiv State Chamber Orchestra augmented by woodwinds, brass and percussion players, as well as drummer Brian Jones and bandura-player Christine Chepyha from Edmonton.

Shumka's music has become remarkably influential across North America. The first dance music album was prepared and released in 1977 and has since been followed by three others. Their quality, especially in light of the lack of material available directly from Ukrainian sources, has made them valuable aids in dance schools across the country.

Musicians play an average of 528 000 notes during a typical performance.

PROFILE:
Gene Zwozdesky

Gene Zwozdesky's first conducting task was a hands-on experience. It occurred while he was a dancer with the troupe, rehearsing for Canada's Centennial celebrations in Ottawa in 1967. Frustrated by the orchestra's tempo, he literally grabbed the baton out of the hand of a bewildered conductor.

Reviewing music parts prior to a performance. From top: Walter Chornowol, Shumka's first music director who still plays the domra for performances; music librarian, Sharon Beckstead; music director Gene Zwozdesky; and bandura-player Christine Chepyha.

Stephen Chwok plays a tsymbaly, a traditional dulcimer-like instrument. Shumka's performances have almost always been accompanied by live music. Today, full orchestral accompaniments are painstakingly developed and supplemented by the sound of authentic Ukrainian instruments.

Gene Zwozdesky is the guiding light for Shumka's music. Working in close collaboration with choreographers, he crafts the orchestral accompaniments that clarify the emotion of each choreographic movement.

"Like this. Like this," he said, waving his arms—and the musicians started to play in time to his motions.

The incident precipitated a contretemps with the shop steward, an all-night session of re-arranging the music, and a twenty-year commitment to Shumka's musical development.

His work as a composer provides the framework of "time" within which choreography occurs. Thanks to Zwozdesky's talent and experience, the framework has become much more flexible than the musical material available to choreographers in the company's early years.

"People back then felt a good deal of frustration as they tried to preserve the integrity of their choreographic ideas within the constraints of the music they had available to them," he recalls.

His years of experience as a dancer and choreographer with the company give him a special rapport with individual dancers on stage, an understanding of their needs, and a sense of responsibility for helping them.

"There's that little extra that the music can do to bring out the best in each dancer's talent and emotion."

His rapport with choreographers is even deeper, built through years of working with artistic directors Orest Semchuk and John Pichlyk to develop the music for story-lines, minute-by-minute and phrase-by-phrase.

Zwozdesky points out that close associations between composers and choreographers are a typical element in developing new dance works. "Petipa and Tchaikovsky left many notes about their collaboration on *The Sleeping Beauty*. While we are always in awe of the classical masters, I'm always aware that, creatively, they faced the same challenges as we do today."

Zwozdesky takes the information provided to him by a choreographer, including the story outline and climaxes, emotions, tempo and the role played by each

This section of the musical score for Enchanted Love *provides the musical expression of the Hag's triumph at successfully stealing Mavka's youth and immortality.*

character in the plot. He identifies or composes appropriate melody lines and selects lead instruments to enhance characterization. Then he writes a preliminary piano score.

This is refined through many more meetings with the choreographer, although the music retains an inner life of its own, with an inherent power to reveal human thoughts and emotions. This ability to express emotion on its own means that music is an essential partner in conveying meaning, not only for an audience but also the dancers themselves.

Many dancers hear only two fundamentals in music: measure and rhythm, says Zwozdesky. However, dancers with a well-developed sense of musicality can find guidance in a score that exceeds what a choreographer can express verbally about characterization and movement.

Zwozdesky's emotional involvement with Ukrainian music is intense, personal, and an integral part of Shumka's success. He has been music arranger/director for a number of dance groups in western Canada, but says the relationship with Shumka is special.

"Shumka affects lives. The more you put into it, the more you get out of it."

The master score for a typical Shumka performance is around 1000 pages long.

STAGE DESIGN

From its earliest days, Shumka has worked hard to create a sense of Ukraine, not only through dancers and costumes, but also through stage design.

The company's set designer and stage manager for concerts in the early years was Wadym Dobrolige, who had studied mural painting and set design at the Academy of Arts in Kyiv. He worked as a set designer and painter in a number of European opera houses and movie studios before coming to Canada in 1948.

His meticulously painted backdrops gave Shumka performances a distinctly professional appearance from the beginning. But as the company began appearing more frequently outside Edmonton, the transportation of heavy sets became a practical problem. Shumka turned to different ways of creating a theatrical sense of place, such as lighting and highly specialized props.

In recent years, the evolving demands of story-lines have posed new challenges to stage design. They require magic crystals that can be seen from the back of a 2000-seat theatre, smoking cauldrons, supernatural beings that grow in front of the audience's eyes. The company has developed a great deal of in-house expertise in staging these special effects. Thanks to people like Gordon Gordey, Shumka has never had to say, "That's not possible" when a story demands magic.

Gordey has turned to top prop- and costume-makers in Canada and the USA, as well as using the most advanced technology available to create effects. The magic crystal used in *A Mother's Tears* for instance, used the light bulbs first used in costumes for the musical *Cats*. The remote control mechanism used to move some of the supernatural beings in *Enchanted Love* is the most advanced equipment of its kind in Canadian theatre.

Masks created by Gail Kennedy help Shumka bring the legends and folk tales of Ukraine to life.

The demands of story-lines have added new challenges to Shumka's staging. Magic crystals and spirit creatures take the best of North American stagecraft to create powerful illusions for the audience. Here, the Hag's brewing bowl for Enchanted Love *requires an ingenious arrangement of flash powder, dry ice, and warm water to foam at the right moments.*

LIVING THE WHIRLWIND

"The Shumka Dancers took the audience with them until two encores and several curtain calls later—they let the curtain fall on our relentless shouts for more. . ."

—Sheri Tillman, Hong Kong TV Times, 1983

CENTRE STAGE:
Performances Over Three Decades

THE CONDUCTOR GIVES the downbeat; the curtain swings aside; a stream of dancers swirls downstage in precise formation. A ripple of anticipation goes through the audience. They are expecting pleasure.

Living the whirlwind over the past thirty years has been above all a series of performances—the peaks that stand out above the busy landscape of rehearsing and stitching costumes and creating choreography. Performance is what Shumka is all about.

Andriy Nahachewsky performs the men's solo step known as "the backbreaker." Performance has been Shumka's raison d'être for the past three decades.

Performance is the high point for which dancers work year-round. Here, the company—dressed in Poltava costume— puts on one of its characteristic displays of colour and motion.

REGULAR PERFORMANCES

The first big concert at Edmonton's Jubilee Auditorium immediately established a tradition. Throughout the 1960s and into the 1970s, the annual concert was the focus for the company's year-round efforts.

From the beginning, guest performers were invited to share the stage with Shumka as a way of providing variety for the audiences and broadening the appeal of dance-only concerts. Early guest artists were very much in the tradition of Ukraine's heritage. Singers such as baritone Domety Berezenetz, soprano Victoria Wynnychuk, or the Dnipro Male Chorus sang Ukrainian folk songs or arias from Ukrainian-inspired operas.

In 1969, this pattern was modified to broaden Shumka's appeal to non-Ukrainian audiences. The Dell Hill Scottish Dancers were invited to share the stage. Over the years, the approach to guest artists became still more varied, as guests such as the Alberta Ballet Company, the folk-rock group Original Caste, and the dance/music group Stratus Faction were invited. This sense of adventure, of crossing boundaries, fitted well with the experimental mood of the early 1970s.

However, the trend created some backlash in the Ukrainian community. Traditional supporters complained that the entertainment was English and it was too loud. They feared Shumka was "forgetting them" and was "only interested in performing for 'strangers.'"

This was not the only area of friction. The practice of scheduling concerts during Lent so students would not have to rehearse during exam period offended the religious sensibilities of some long-time Shumka supporters.

Concerns like these were taken seriously by the group, to the point where the executive approached the bishop of each denomination to receive dispensation to hold concerts during Lent. Nevertheless, members of the company felt instinctively that they were on the right track and their intention of taking Ukrainian dance to a wider audience paid off. Concerts where non-Ukrainian entertainers shared the stage were highly successful and Shumka's ticket sales grew steadily.

CONVENTIONS, KLONDIKE DAYS, AND CLUB DATES

While the annual concert was the company's main creative focus, Shumka's popularity and professionalism created a demand for their lively art form. Almost immediately, the company was being asked to do concerts for local occasions.

In the first year after Shumka's founding in 1959, for instance, the group performed for audiences as diverse as the Catholic Women's League convention at the McDonald Hotel, the Derrick Golf & Country Club, and the Edmonton Norwood Social Credit constituency association.

"Local" soon came to include almost all of north-central Alberta. From opening the Westlock Jubilee Family Recreation Centre to performing for the Smoky Lake/Lamont Hospital Auxiliary benefit, Shumka performed in many communities throughout central Alberta in the 1960s.

Brief shows to entertain people at conventions or other special events also became a constant feature of Shumka's performance record. It seemed everyone wanted to see the Shumka dancers—from the recreation ministers of Canada to the Propane Gas Association to the organizers of Edmonton's Klondike Days festival.

For $250, the Alberta Contract Bridge Club enjoyed half an hour of colour and dance. Although individual dancers were not paid for these performances, the fees helped cover for the troupe's expenses and subsidize other activities. Even more importantly, the performances kept the company in front of audiences year-round, building an enthusiastic base for larger concerts.

CROSSING BORDERS:
Tours in Canada and Abroad

It was only a matter of time before Shumka's horizons broadened beyond northern Alberta. The seeds were sown in the mid-1960s, when Shumka joined the Alberta Folk Arts Council, an organization dedicated to making audiences aware of the richness and variety of the province's multicultural heritage.

On national and international stages, much of Shumka's popularity with audiences has been due to spectacular displays by male dancers. Dennis Elkow's "threading-the-needle" was a favourite hopak solo from Tunis to Hong Kong. Photo: Con Boland.

Through the Folk Arts Council, Shumka was approached to appear at Expo '67 as part of the biggest arts program ever held in conjunction with a world fair. This trip included appearances in Ottawa and Hull, and led to standing ovations from audiences who had never seen Shumka's type of entertainment before. The Expo performances in front of thousands of people were an intense emotional experience for the company. They felt as though they were now living up to the expectations, not only of their local community, but also of Canada.

In 1969, the Folk Arts Council organized a troupe to tour Tunisia. Organizer Nena Temperley invited Shumka to send ten dancers with a company of fifty-five Canadian artists that made up a collage of ethnic groups. This Canadian entry to the Tunis festival was awarded fifth place among entries from all over the world.

During this first tour abroad, the Shumka participants watched on a grainy black-and-white television in a Tunis hotel as astronaut Neil Armstrong became the first human being to set foot on the moon. It seemed to them that their own journey had taken them almost as far.

RETHINKING THE ANNUAL CONCERT

By 1974 it had become apparent to the executive that the group could no longer do a major show every year at the Jubilee Auditorium. Not only were costs high, but the time was simply inadequate to pull together a completely new and exciting performance, especially since the executive had decided to experiment with a show that did not feature guest artists, who had previously filled about half of the program.

In March 1975, Shumka performed its first two-hour production without guest artists. That production was also the first Shumka would take outside Alberta. A performance in Winnipeg's Centennial Centre Concert Hall was staged in addition to the customary performances in Edmonton and Calgary.

Seats were sold out and the crowd was wildly enthusiastic, although the executive realized that a one-time performance could not possibly recoup the costs of travelling and staging the show. Nevertheless, the idea of taking the regular concert on tour became fixed.

Around this time, Shumka began going even further afield. Recognizing the group's potential as a cultural ambassador, Alberta's then-minister of culture, Horst Schmid, encouraged Shumka's participation in a 1974 exchange with Japan. Tom Stefanyk, Vlad Eshenko, and Dennis Elkow went as part of a larger multicultural troupe. A similar cultural exchange took Gerry Wowk and Orest Semchuk to Korea in 1975.

Shumka was next invited by Fujita Enterprises of Japan to perform for four weeks in the resort town of Hakone. In 1976 a group of twenty-six singers and dancers, along with musicians Teddy Borowiecki and Walter Chornowol, performed there. The trip was an

Shumka first took its energy abroad in 1969, when ten dancers formed part of a group representing Canada at an international festival in Tunisia. Dancers prepare to rehearse in the ancient amphitheatre of Carthage as part of the Tunisia tour.

unforgettable experience for those able to participate, demonstrating clearly the international appeal of dance across different languages and cultures.

In fact, the appeal was so great that Shumka was invited a third time to Japan in 1977. During a layover in Hawaii on their return, they appeared on the Don Ho television variety show.

In 1976, another tradition was established. Vlad Eshenko, one of the many Shumka members who also taught Ukrainian dancing in church schools around central and northern Alberta, urged that these young students be recognized and rewarded. He suggested that a concert at the Jubilee Auditorium be held in off-years when the company was not staging one of its major concerts. This event, known familiarly as the "Kiddies

Show," is held at the Jubilee Auditorium. It gives children who take lessons from Shumka members the chance to show off their skills, accompanied by an orchestra, for a huge live audience.

HEADS OF STATE AND STATE AFFAIRS

While performances for Legion celebrations and the opening of shopping centres were still important community events, Shumka was becoming a must-have at prominent affairs, to perform for national and international audiences.

The first Canada Day appearance in 1967 had led to others. In 1977 their performance in front of the Parliament Buildings missed being rained out by a hair;

A highlight of the mid-1970s was an invitation to visit Japan and perform at the resort town of Hakone. Back row, from left: Vlad Eshenko, Gerry Wowk, Teddy Borowieki, Tom Stefanyk, Bill Baziuk, John Eshenko, Bohdan Maslo, Michael Sulyma, Walter Chornowol. Middle row: Loverne Wowk, Shirley Doskoch, Darleen Bohnet; Betty Corlett; MaryAnn Baziuk, Audrey Morello, Lorrie Sulyma; Halyna Elkow. Front row: Terry Mucha; Maria Van Steenoven, Dennis Elkow, Linda Maslo, Marilyn Mucha.

Shumka stepped onto the national stage when the company was asked to perform for Canada's Centennial celebrations in 1967 in front of the Parliament Building. Since then, the company has frequently been asked to return to celebrate Canada Day in Ottawa. Here, dancers rehearse their 1977 performance. This particular show was directed by John Hirsch, who described Shumka as "a national treasure."

Members of the Shumka cast are greeted and congratulated by Her Majesty, Queen Elizabeth II, after a gala performance in Edmonton. The company has performed for virtually every Canadian prime minister since it was founded, as well as foreign dignitaries such as USA President Ronald Reagan.

in 1978 Shumka was the only ethno-cultural group invited. "Being so prominent a part of Canada's national birthday made me enormously proud," recalls Bill Baziuk, who danced at all the Canada Day celebrations.

In 1978, the company spent days rehearsing in pouring rain for the opening celebrations of the Commonwealth Games at Edmonton's new Commonwealth Stadium. They danced finally in sunshine, knowing that the world was watching.

That same year brought a command performance for Queen Elizabeth II at the Citadel Theatre. Added to the thrill of audience response was the opportunity to talk to Her Majesty afterwards.

"I don't know how the others felt, but I actually had a huge lump in my throat," recalls Halyna Elkow.

In 1982, an engraved invitation from the Secretary of State informed invitees that they would be in the Queen's company once again. A gala performance at the National Arts Centre was staged to celebrate one of the most significant developments in the country's history: the patriation of Canada's constitution. The dancers were awed by the prestigious audience out front—and just as awed backstage by performers like Evelyn Hart and David Peregrine of the Royal Winnipeg Ballet. Celebrated contralto Maureen Forrester reassured them that everything would be "just great."

In fact, this was the second time that Shumka had appeared before a head of state on the National Arts Centre stage. The previous year, a gala performance had been televised on the occasion of a visit to Ottawa by President Ronald Reagan. During a production meeting on this show, orchestra leader Tommy Banks was asked, "Where should we put Shumka on the program?"

His response: "I replied that they had to be put last, because nobody can possibly follow a Shumka performance."

ON THE ROAD AGAIN . . .

As the years passed, Shumka's tours became more complex. With every tour a few more performances were added, a few more cities visited, the budget increased. By 1987, the budget was nearing $1 million. Tour producer Michael Sulyma's log showed that he spent more than 220 days of volunteer time to produce the show.

The grants and subsidies available to professional dance companies have never been available to Shumka—even though Shumka ranks fifth among Canadian dance companies in terms of ticket sales, in spite of its short touring season. When the company first performed in Toronto in 1982, the 3250-seat O'Keefe Centre was sold out, along with the standing-room-only spaces.

To compensate, the company has worked hard to obtain other kinds of funding, particularly from the corporate sector. In the mid-1980s, members of the executive initiated a vigorous campaign in the office towers of Bay Street. This led to Air Canada's generous sponsorship of air travel for the 1987 tour, recognizing Shumka's combination of volunteer dedication and professional calibre performance.

"It was quite a coup for an amateur company," Sulyma says.

By far the bulk of the company's financial base is made up through the passionate willingness of the members themselves. If Shumka were to pay for the volunteer services it receives from dancers and production staff, its budget would be second only to the National Ballet of Canada.

"Amateur" is a word often contrasted unfavourably with "professional," implying a lesser artistic offering from people willing to accept lower standards. But to the professionals who have dealt with Shumka over the years, the word "amateur" shines out with its meaning rooted in the Latin word *amo*, "I love." The dancers who set such high standards for themselves do it from love.

In Tommy Banks's words, "Among people in my trade, Shumka's reputation is for excellence . . . They've never been late, they've never been down and they've never failed to dazzle."

PROFILE: John Pichlyk

John Pichlyk, Shumka's current artistic director, joined the company in 1976. Almost immediately, he demonstrated the enthusiasm and creativity that led him to assume Orest Semchuk's position in 1982, when Semchuk indicated that he wanted to phase himself out of the artistic director's role. Today, Pichlyk's

Vivacity and precision ensure that female dancers take their turn at centre stage. From left: Nadine Samycia, Maria Chrunik, and Alana Prytuluk.

stubborn conviction of Shumka's artistic potential has placed an indelible stamp on the company.

He started his own dance training relatively late. As a grade ten student at St. Vladimir's College in Roblin, Manitoba, he found himself drafted into the dance section for the school's year-end fund-raising concert. However, having discovered dance, he embraced it with a characteristic passion that eventually drove him to New York, and to Ukraine to study with the renowned Virsky school.

His early training, as for most young people learning Ukrainian dance in North America, was based on the repertoire of dances originally taught by Vasile Avramenko. Pichlyk was also strongly influenced by teachers he encountered later in New York, like Roma Pryma-Bohachevsky and Vadym Sulyma. He said Bohachevsky was "the ultimate example for me of how the principles of classical training could improve the art of Ukrainian dance." And "Sulyma taught me that a great dancer had to be able to dance with the deer's grace but also with the tiger's strength."

As artistic director, Orest Semchuk had stressed the importance of togetherness and working precisely as a corps. Pichlyk challenges the dancers to develop their individual capabilities to the utmost. Achieving the full potential of Ukrainian dance requires "a blending of the individual's physical and emotional skills," he says. Individual dancers must have the physical training needed to carry out a movement and a deep understanding of its emotional significance. Both aspects are essential if meaning is to be conveyed clearly and precisely to an audience.

During a single Shumka performance, forty-five dancers cover approximately 225 km as they go through their choreography.

Ultimately, dancers must work together on stage within the context of an overall pattern. But every individual has to find his or her way of expressing the overall pattern. In Pichlyk's analogy, the goal is similar to the interaction of light in a rainbow: to see the individual colours in the final whole.

"I think in every individual there is an undiscovered fulfillment that is trying to get out," he says. He proceeds to pull this undiscovered fulfillment out of people, even when they didn't realize it was there—and even when the process isn't altogether comfortable.

He stresses the importance of alignment and musicality. "Dancers have to learn to feel the music, not just keep time." He also emphasizes the use of classic principles from disciplines like character dance to emphasize movements.

Another creative priority has been the development of Shumka's musical arrangements to meet the needs of choreography and develop characters. In developing story-lines, he works intensively with accompanists such as Teddy Borowiecki and Valerian Markevych to develop musical themes that music director Gene Zwozdesky will then orchestrate.

Disciplined—to the point of fanaticism, some say—obsessed, inspiring, and creative, he is a demanding artistic director.

"Pichlyk was a lot of fun to work with, but he was tough. My body still hasn't forgiven him," says one ex-dancer.

His greatest strength is pushing a vision out ahead of the company.

"John can see things—what the finished dance or a specific movement will look like—before we can. It's so wonderful once the company gets to his level, when I can see and feel for myself what he knew all along could happen," says another dancer.

Pichlyk's vision shares the deep respect for his heritage with all Shumka's artistic directors. He sees Ukrainian dance as a means of expressing a universal human spirit that transcends boundaries.

"That spirit is centuries old. It won't change if Shumka comes or goes—we are a stepping stone to something greater. The next generation will take that same spirit and portray it in a different way," he says.

While he can't help pushing the boundaries, he also acknowledges the requirement for authenticity.

"It's like the ten commandments. You've got to have a standard of conduct that can overrule your personal choreographic desires. Otherwise, you're not portraying *Ukrainian* dance."

Shumka dancers create a sweep of colour onstage that is dazzling and professional. But these professionals also hold other full-time jobs. The time and energy they give to Shumka is entirely voluntary.

John Pichlyk works with John Zinchuk to shape the emotion of a scene for Enchanted Love.

As artistic director, John Pich-lyk's priority is to develop the dancers' emotional skills as well as their physical abilities. Here, he works with Alana Prytyluk to demonstrate the emotion behind a gesture.

TO BE A DANCER

To be involved in Shumka over the past three decades has, almost inevitably, meant being a dancer. To be a dancer is to be just about everything else as well—choreographer, costume designer, fundraiser, tour producer. The traditional dividing lines between performers, artistic creators, and administrative staff have always been blurred in the Shumka operation.

Dancers contributed 3500 volunteer hours to preparing for the 1991 Canadian Concert Tour.

A choreographer is "anyone who has an idea," said Orest Semchuk in an interview in the early 1970s.

"Somebody will come to a practice one time and say, 'You know I was watching a TV show and I got an idea for a dance.' Or, 'I heard some Ukrainian music that somebody found somewhere and I thought of a dance to go with it.' And they'll teach it."

That approach to creating dances has remained characteristic of Shumka. Artistic teamwork—formalized through the establishment of the artistic committee—plays an important role in planning and developing new works.

Perhaps it is not surprising that formal divisions between dancing and creating dances are not made by Shumka. What is surprising is that the traditional division between artistic and administrative tasks was never made either. Dancers pay monthly bills, make boots, stitch costumes and make tour bookings. Not until 1984 did the company hire a professional publicist for the first time to promote its tour.

"Shumka has always been fortunate in having people with artistic abilities as well as administrative and business skills," says Gene Zwozdesky, who himself combined dancing with musical direction for many years.

This broad range of abilities is available to the company largely because its members are all volunteers. In their day-to-day lives, they may be accountants, travel agents, secretaries, teachers, students, industrial workers, doctors or film producers, with a wealth of knowledge and practical experience that has been worth a fortune to Shumka over the years.

The broad participation also binds the group together.

"When every decision—artistic, financial, and administrative—is made by the dancers themselves, you get an amazing level of support," points out Gordon Gordey. A dancer himself for seventeen years, Gordon has thrown himself into every aspect of the company's activities.

He points out there is a price to pay for this collective approach. The drain on time and energy is immense.

"I try not to remember the long weekend planning retreats. Instead, I just focus on the closeness we all developed."

Shumka's creativity is a collaborative process in which dancers are also choreographers, costume designers, and stage managers. The artistic committee that developed the 1987 tour program, from left: John Pichlyk, Annette Bidniak, Natalka Beaudoin, Terry Mucha and George Chrunik.

The Shumka company assembles for pryvit *during the 1984 tour. Few members of the audience at a Shumka perform-ance realize that the dancers onstage also carry out all the company's backstage duties, from raising funds to making props.*

REHEARSE, REHEARSE, REHEARSE

The volunteer nature of the company means that its members have to be, if anything, *more* dedicated than the members of a professional dance company in order to achieve the performance standards that Shumka has always set.

Each dancer spends more than 450 hours rehearsing and performing during the year of a major tour.

Monday night rehearsals were established almost from the beginning—although Shumka could never count on having the same school gymnasium for rehearsals for more than a few months at a time. Dancers who used public transit learned bus routes all over the city.

The demands of rehearsal time were substantial: three hours a night, three nights a week to prepare for a concert. Some members of the troupe would drive 200 km to attend, do their homework in the car, eat on the go and get home at one in the morning.

"In a show year, the only excuse for missing rehearsal is DEATH," says Marion Ostapchuk, who danced from 1960 to 1974.

A rehearsal dress code was established in the early 1970s: black tights, a Shumka T-shirt and slippers. The drill for rehearsals was also well established: a half-hour warm-up led by Orest Semchuk or Gerry Wowk. Orest's style was quiet, but if the warm-up was led by Wowk, "the rest of the evening your ears would just buzz with the after-effect."

The commitment extended beyond the dancers to their families. Parents drove their children in from communities like Two Hills and Andrew for the thrice-weekly rehearsals. They helped sell *pyrohy* at shopping malls to raise funds; they helped embroider costumes and paint scenery. Families missed troupe members at dinners and on special occasions because of rehearsals. Michael Sulyma, Michael Taciuk, and Marilyn Mucha gave up attending their university graduation ceremonies to perform in Winnipeg.

FAMILY FEELING

To become a Shumka dancer was to acquire a new family, and its members became as closely knit as blood relations.

In the first two decades, many of the Shumka members went to school together and lived near each other. They often married other dancers and stood as godparents to one another's children. The result was a very stable troupe, where dancers stayed for ten, twelve, fifteen years.

One demonstration of this long, close association occurred when Shumka danced at the silver wedding

Greg Zukiwsky whirls Natalka Beaudoin (Stus) during her wedding celebrations. The intense family feeling developed as part of the Shumka experience leads to lifelong friendships.

of Leo and Mary Zalucky in 1984. The Zaluckys had been among the founding dancers of Shumka. Their marriage in 1959 had been the first to take place between two members and it was followed by others.

The bonds of hard work and performance were reinforced by shared fun—shaving-cream fights, parties where the girls danced the male roles and vice-versa, sing-songs to while away long train or bus rides. The executive established a strict ban on alcohol for twenty-four hours before a performance, but the after-performance parties went until dawn.

Social bonds were paralleled by equally close artistic bonds.

"A lot of the stuff that goes on between creative people after they've been working together for twenty years—frequently, you don't use words. You just know instinctively." says Gene Zwosdesky, recalling his rapport with artistic director Orest Semchuk.

It would be naive to assume that every moment was friendship and camaraderie, that there were never disagreements or frustrations, that some people didn't occasionally feel on the outside of a tightly knit core. But on the whole, the people who have been part of the organization over the years say that to be a Shumka dancer has been the most intensely rewarding experience of their lives.

Change is inevitable, and Shumka's silver anniversary year in 1984 marked a watershed in the membership. Part of this was due to a natural aging process, as many dancers who had been with the company for ten or fifteen years left to be replaced by younger people. Many of these departing dancers remained closely involved with the organization. This involvement was formalized by the formation of the Ukrainian Shumka Dancers Alumni Association in 1984.

At the same time, dancers are now expected to have ten years of dance training before coming to the company. Many now look to Shumka as an avenue that will further a professional dance career. This may affect the length of time that dancers are willing to stay with the company.

"A larger commitment over a shorter time period is a natural pattern," says Pichlyk.

However, he feels Shumka will continue to attract and hold dancers because of the profile it has and the opportunities it offers—opportunities that still include the chance to share experiences that are as intense and fulfilling as ever. The dancers who went to Ukraine were a relatively young corps, but the challenges of the tour drew them together quickly and firmly.

Tracy Metrunec recalls her best memory of Ukraine: watching one particular performance of *pryvit*, the traditional welcome of bread and salt.

"Usually I watch it as a group of people, but today I saw them all as individuals—people I care for and love. It was just such a great thing to see us as a family."

TEACHING FOR TOMORROW:
The Shumka School of Ukrainian Dance

Teaching each new generation the tradition and the joy of Ukrainian dance has been a responsibility taken seriously since the days of Vasile Avramenko. Today, approximately 4000 students study Ukrainian dance throughout the province of Alberta. Included in this number are sixty-five young people enroled in the Shumka School of Ukrainian Dance.

The Shumka School held its first classes in 1989. It was established for several reasons. First, it was seen as an opportunity to direct young dancers towards Shumka and help ensure that the company will have the talent and enthusiasm to continue.

Secondly, the school is designed to make the transition into the company easier and smoother by training students in the distinctive elements of Shumka's style. These include not only the traditional basics as interpreted by Shumka, but also training in the other disciplines required by the company, such as character, barre, and story-line choregraphy.

Finally, the school emerged in response to strong public demand from students who want to learn what Shumka has to offer.

The school currently holds classes at three levels. Students must have some previous instruction in Ukrainian dance and be at least twelve years old to enrol, although age does not necessarily determine the class level a pupil enters.

The tradition continues: young dancers show off their skills during the 1990 Ukrainian Dancing Schools in Concert performance at Edmonton's Jubilee Auditorium. The concert gives hundreds of dance students taught by members of Shumka an opportunity to take part in a full-scale production, complete with live orchestra. The "Kiddies' Show," as it is called informally, has been a Shumka tradition since 1976. It is part of the company's commitment to ensure that the joy and energy of Ukrainian dance reaches each new generation—a commitment that is also evident in the founding of Shumka's own dance school in 1989.

Erin Corlett awaits her turn on stage. Today, approximately 4000 students study Ukrainian dance throughout the province of Alberta.

The curriculum places a strong emphasis on perfecting the basics of Ukrainian dance says Dorianne Martyniuk, one of the school's three instructors.

"The basics are basic. You never stop rehearsing them."

However, each year the students have the opportunity to choreograph and perform their own dance material publicly.

As new generations of dancers come along, it appears that Ukrainian dance is becoming more a part of Canada's mainstream culture, if enrolment in the Shumka School is any indication. The instructors are seeing more students who are not of Ukrainian origin but who are attracted by the exuberance of the art form. Ukrainian dance has been added to ballet, tap, and jazz by a number of Alberta dance schools, and is a favourite with male students in particular.

The future is bright, in terms of general interest in Ukrainian dance training and for the Shumka school. The possibility of opening the school to younger students and of expanding the curriculum has already been considered and will be re-evaluated regularly says Martyniuk.

"The demand is certainly there," she says. "The only question is, when is the right time to take that next step?"

UKRAINE TOUR

"At the end of that first show in Kyiv . . . even though my body was incredibly tired, the only thing that really ached was my heart. We were dancing for our relatives and strangers in our homeland. They were clapping so loudly. We had given our all—my heart just ached."

- Greg Zukiwsky

Exhausted by forty hours in planes and airports . . . missing their artistic director . . . awed by the splendour of Kyiv's Taras Shevchenko opera house, with its crushing weight of tradition and artistry . . . wrestling with the last-minute crises of lighting cues . . . adjusting to an unfamiliar, sloping stage that caught the dancers' heels in their rehearsal skirts and threw off the angle of jumps . . .

It was a miracle the opening concert of Shumka's Ukraine tour didn't blow a fuse. Instead, the tensions created an electric current that looped the performers into a whole and reached out to encircle the audience.

Applause, ovation, flowers, flowers, flowers —the opening in Kyiv set the pattern for the whole tour of Ukraine.

The Taras Shevchenko Theatre of Opera and Ballet, Kyiv—another breathtaking stage for Shumka.

OLD DREAMS, LONG NEGOTIATIONS

The dream of taking Shumka's artistry back to the homeland was decades old. It had been talked of almost as long as Shumka had been in existence, and had been a personal vision for artistic director John Pichlyk after his trip to study in Ukraine in 1980.

Over the years, prohibitive costs and political barriers prevented it from being realized. But the reality started to crystallize after Shumka's performance at the 1988 Olympics in Calgary, when the company was invited to share the stage with the Soviet Ukrainian Bandura Chorus.

There was much soul-searching over this opportunity. The old nationalist, anti-communist emotions still ran deep in Edmonton's Ukrainian community. But eventually, the company decided that it would make a better statement by appearing with the Bandura Chorus in the non-political framework of an Olympic celebration than by refusing.

The decision proved to be the stepping stone that made the Ukraine tour a reality. The impressario who had arranged the Bandura Chorus tour, John Cripton, had arranged numerous other visits by Soviet performers like the Red Army Chorus and the Kirov Ballet.

Negotiations were long and often frustrating for producer Michael Sulyma and the others involved. Early promises of "anything you want" ran head to head with the fact that the Soviet organizers had no idea why Shumka needed the kind of facilities it wanted. The Soviets could not understand why, for instance, the company could not perform in a theatre with no orchestra pit or in a soccer stadium.

For the Ukraine tour, Shumka had to pack costumes, props, and equipment that weighed 4800 pounds and filled the equivalent of a 10 m tractor-trailer.

The tour was postponed several times, creating artistic problems as dancers came and went and people had to learn new roles. Funding also presented the usual challenge for Shumka. While the Soviet sponsors, Rosconcert, would cover expenses in Ukraine, the company was still responsible for paying costs for pre-production, travel, shipment of props and insurance. The bills would be nearly $250 000.

Members of the alumni association threw their energies into helping with a fund-raising campaign that included gala performances and raffles, as well as funding requests to municipal and provincial sources. Dancing in Ukraine was a dream they had shared during their own time with Shumka, and they were anxious to help make it come true for the company in 1990.

Once the tour date was finalized, things didn't get easier. Dancers and organizers were trying to manage regular jobs as well as full eight- and ten-hour days rehearsing, preparing props and costumes, and coordinating the immense amount of administrative detail required.

In the final months, Pichlyk was called away several times by his father's terminal illness. At the last minute, he found he would not be able to leave with the rest of the company.

On the day of the departure, Pichlyk saw the troupe off from Edmonton's international airport with a heartfelt farewell.

"Just remember everything comes from the heart, through the eyes and then finally into the feet," he told them. "I'll catch up with you in Lviv if I can."

THE UKRAINE EXPERIENCE

"Sixty-four people went over there. Sixty-four changed people came back," says Michael Sulyma.

The changes were partly due to the challenges of pulling off a North-American style of production in the teeth of a completely different culture. It was, in Sulyma's words, "crisis management every day."

One ongoing crisis was posed by the limitations of Soviet technical equipment. Sometimes, there weren't enough electric circuits to light the whole show and the dance patterns had to be adjusted to compensate. Amplifiers blew.

"I've never seen so much hot wiring in my life," says music director Gene Zwozdesky. He was himself wrestling with musicians who—however well trained— were not used to sight-reading for travelling concerts.

At one point, the computer program governing lighting cues crashed. Gordon Gordey and his technicians had to re-program seventy-five lighting cues with only an hour to go before the opening performance.

The lack of consumer goods and services taken for granted in North America created other challenges. Without machine washers and dryers, costumes had to be hand-washed in sinks and hung in the dancers' rooms to dry. A resourceful driver who was driving the props trailer to Moscow made the last leg of the journey only by trading a length of garlic sausage for enough gasoline to finish.

It was virtually impossible to telephone to Canada. By the time a call was placed, the company had moved to another hotel and the arduous process of connecting with the long-distance system had to begin all over again. Water and food were unfamiliar, and the dancers couldn't help thinking wistfully of home.

"Dancing was one of the easiest parts of touring the Soviet Union. It was the thing that felt most like home," recalls Sheryl Passek.

However, even dancing was not altogether easy.

The exhilaration of performing for audiences in Ukraine lent an even greater vigour to the dancers—in spite of performing their opening concert in Kyiv shortly after forty hours of delay in airports.

From left: Lorraine Chanasyk, Shelley Borowski and Natalka Prytylyk in Hutsul costume. Dancing on the unfamiliar, angled stages of the opera houses was a challenge. The offstage challenges of the tour were even greater as the company adjusted to Soviet technical standards and the lack of consumer goods and services that are taken for granted in North America.

The angled stages of the big opera houses felt completely different from dancing on a flat stage.

"You get your momentum going downstage and you can't stop, and then you're dancing upstage and it's like running uphill," says Roxanne MacLean.

Overcoming the technical challenges and differences in culture pulled the troupe together and created a bond among its members. But if people came back from Ukraine changed, it was not so much because of the difficulties. It was because of the intense emotional experience of giving back Shumka's Ukrainian dance to the people who had originated it.

"John Pichlyk had always talked about the kinds of feelings you should experience when dancing *pryvit*. But I never truly felt them until we performed in Ukraine," says Jennifer MacLean. "I felt the audience knew and understood the importance and the tradition of *pryvit* . . . because of this, it almost felt as if my heart would burst every time I performed it."

Ukrainian audiences included not only artistic people but also many thousands of "regular folks," says Laurel Chomyc. "They know exactly what we're doing and why we're doing it. There's nothing like dancing here because it's *their* dance."

"The Ukrainian tour had an emotional impact that was different from other tours, deeper, more intense," says Dorianne Martyniuk, who has performed with Shumka in many special performances, including those before Ronald Reagan and at the Olympic games.

"I've never felt more proud to be Canadian than I did on stage in Ukraine."

The emotion swept up everyone, from Viktor Stepovy who had grown up in Kyiv and learned to dance there, to people who had no personal experience of Ukraine at all. For many dancers, the Ukraine tour brought about rapturous reunions with families who had been strangers for years or even generations.

"It was a remarkable experience," says Darka Cherkawsky who arrived in Lviv to be greeted at the railway station by six aunts and uncles and nine cousins whom she had never before met.

"It was really wonderful to come that way—not as a visitor or a tourist," she adds. "We were showing

them what we'd done with the roots that many of them thought we had lost."

For every member of the troupe, there is some picture, whether onstage or off, that sums up the emotional intensity of the Ukraine tour and the bond it created with an ancient heritage. For one, it was the sense of tranquility felt in a visit to the Carpathian Mountains—a sense that her Baba, long-dead, was with her for a moment and proud. For another, it was the sight of the opera house in Kyiv; for many it was the warm applause sweeping up and over the stage.

To look offstage in Ivano-Frankivsk and see an old woman weeping as she watched . . . to see the Ukrainian flag hung proudly from a balcony during one of the performances in Kyiv . . . to visit a church in Lviv just being reopened after decades . . . to feel the stubborn survival of the heritage that Shumka expresses in dance and music and story . . . . In some way, these diverse experiences justified what Shumka has tried to do artistically over the years to preserve a heritage and communicate it in new ways.

Accolades from dancers in Ukraine and invitations to have Shumka members visit Ukrainian dance companies to provide a creative spark have also given the troupe a sense that their innovations do fit within the framework of their heritage.

The tour "has given us confidence to believe in our direction," says Pichlyk.

The tour was not only an occasion for pride in the group's Ukrainian heritage. In equally strong degree, it defined for them their Canadian identity.

During the last performance in Moscow, the dancers looked around in surprise to see Todd Safronovich carrying a Canadian flag for the final *hopak*.

"I was proud to be Ukrainian—but I have never been so emotionally attached to Canada as I was at that moment," says Kathleen Todoruk, echoing the emotion felt by the whole company.

As Safronovich was tossed through the air in the dance, the flag streamed behind him. For Shumka, it was a symbol of joyous identification with the country to which their ancestors had immigrated in search of peace, dignity, and freedom—including the freedom to dance.

Dorianne Martyniuk hugs one of her fellow dancers after a performance. Intense emotion was a hallmark of the Ukraine tour, both onstage and off, as many of the dancers met long-lost family members for the first time.

The curtain of the Ivano-Franko Theatre in Lviv, with its gold threads and allegorical painting of "Parnassus," is valued at millions.

Ukrainian audiences responded enthusiastically to innovations such as the fantasy love duet from Enchanted Love. *The balance between preserving Ukrainian traditions accurately and presenting them in new ways has been a major challenge throughout Shumka's history. However, the Ukraine tour gave the company renewed confidence in its approach.*

George Chrunik expresses another emotion that was characteristic of the Ukraine tour: a deep pride in being Canadian.

APPENDIX

MEMBERS PAST AND PRESENT

More than 300 dancers have been part of the Ukrainian Shumka Dancers since the company was founded in 1959. A book such as this can mention relatively few individuals by name, but every member of the company played an important part in making Shumka's history—and every dancer would have his or her *own* history to write about the experience.

PAST MEMBERS

Halia Achtemichuk (Melnychuk)
Gwen Andruik
Lorraine Antonello (Proch)
Paul Barlott
Bill Baziuk**
MaryAnn Baziuk (Chorney) ☆
Natalka Beaudoin (Stus)
Wendy Beisel (Samycia)
Annette Bidniak
Donna Bihun (Topolnisky)
Helen Binette (Stechishin)
Irene Bladon (Warnick)
Bill Blazuk
Connie Bobei (Nilsson)
Joe Bodnar
Rev. Peter Bodnar
Darleen Bohnet (Panasiuk)*
Marie Bootsman (Horobec)

Leona Bridges (Faryna)
Tasha Broome (Kaminsky)
Lauren Burke (Lundquist)
Pat Carrow (Pelech)
Ray Charuk
Mike Choloniwsky
Maria Chrunik (Trach)
George Chrunik
Max Chorney
Iris Ciona (Zwozdesky)
Betty Corlett (Mukanik) ☆
Elaine Dasko
Eugene Dejneka
Chris Dewald (Balko)
Oksana Dexter (Jendyk)
Natalka Dobrolige
Roxanne Dohm (Moroz)
Lil Dorash (Fedorow)
Shirley Doskoch
Eugene Dub
Lora Duchnij (Turgeon)
Joan Duff (Fedorow)
Sherry Dyck
Joan Dymianiw
Michael Dzenick
Tim Dzenick
Dennis Elkow**
Halyna Elkow (Prokopchuk) ☆
Okcana Ensslen (Chomiak)
John Eshenko
Luba Eshenko

Vlad Eshenko* ☆
Dennis Ewasiuk
Betty Faryna (Topolnitsky)
Myron Faryna
Peter Fedorow
Michael Fedyna
Kirsten Feldberg
Dave Ferbey
Susan Ferbey
Orest Fialka
Borys Flak
Chris Forth (Ewasiuk)
Lesia Foty (Yusypchuk)
Dianne Fyk (Proniuk)†
Troy Gaboury
Lydia Galas (Eshenko)
Cyrene Gander (Stefanyk)
Eleanor Gasparik (Janis)
Gordon Gordey**
Blain Gowing ☆
Marlene Gowing (Sulyma)
Michele Gray
Gail Grekel
Connie Grimsrud (Ewanishan)
Karen Grummett (Pawluski)
Linda Harasim
Darcia Hasey (Ponich)
Catherine Hauptman
Lilia Hawrish (Baziuk)
Eugene Hirniak
Bob Hladun
Irene Hoblak (Melnychuk)
Rev. Demjan Hohol'
Keenan Hohol'
Nona Holden (Pylypiuk)†
Valerie Horan (Klimchuk)
Michael Horban
Kevin Iszcenko
Toby Iszcenko
Sven Izio
Mike Janis
George Jendyk
Elaine Jephcott (Hale)
Vivian Johnson (Nikiforuk)
Barbara Johnson
Mary Kalynsky
John Kaminski

Roger Kaminsky
Barry Karpiak
Lawrence Kenakin
Mike Klapey
Rose Klapey
Rodney Klimchuk
Khrystyna Kohut (Yopuk)
Darry Kolonsky
Pat Kolotyluk (Proniuk)
Steve Koper
Anna-Marie Kosarycz (Kryschuk)
Paul Kowal
Donna Kowalishin (Ewasiuk)
Donna Kozak
Nadia Kramar
Nadia Kreptul
Joe Kryschuk
Karen Kryschuk (Kupchenko)
Chester Kuc**
Lorna Kunyk (Salamandick)
Dwayne Kushniruk
Orest Kuszka
Irene Kuszka
Audrey Kuzyk
Pat Kuzyk
Alex Kyselytzia
Steffany Kyselytzia (Puchyr)
Sharon Laskiwski
Sally Lazaruk
Judy Leith (Shewchuk)
Darlene Letain (Kassian)
Orysia Luchak
Oleh Lukomskyj
Patricia Lychak
Betty Macyk (Pelech)
Ed Macyk
Helene Magus
George Majiwskyj
Marianne Makowsky (Baziuk)
Bill Malmo
Shannon Maluzynsky (Hohol')
Roman Manastersky
Luba Manley (Stangret)
Mary Anne Manning (Zaddery)
Dorianne Martyniuk (Slipchuk)
Bohdan Maslo
Linda Maslo (Welokochy)

Marianna Maslo
Nestor Maslo
Irene McMillan (Choloniwsky)
Linda McWilliam (Daciuk)
Gerald Metrunec**
Earl Misanchuk
Audrey Morello (Melnychuk) ☆
Pat Morency (Nykolyn)
Donna Moroz
Marcia Moroz
John Mucha
Marilyn Mucha
Michele Mucha (Warawa)
Terry Mucha-Lynn* ☆
Andriy Nahachewsky
Kim Nahachewsky
Lawrence Niniowsky
Marcee Niniowsky
Irene Olijnyk (Mandryk)
Anne-Marie Ongaro (Lamoureux)
George Orlecki
Gregory Orysiuk
Lesia Osoba
Gordon Ostapchuk
Marion Ostapchuk (Fedorow)
Cathy Ozubko-Aspden
Don Palylyk
Ken Palylyk
Don Panchuk
Irena Pankiw (Halko)
Dianne Parker (Sawchyn)
Maria Pawlowski
Martha Pawluk
Johann Pelech
Evelyn Piush
Lecia Polujan
Nadine Porisky
Peter Poznansky
Morris Pritz
Michael Prokopiw
Dave Pysyk
Kathy Rhodes
Zoria Robinson (Lytwyn)
Susan Romaniuk (Zinchuk)
Dianne Ross (Kraychy)
Dave Rudyk
Marilyn Rulka (Winnick)

Lori Ruptash (Chmelyk)
Sharon Ruptash (Fedyna)
Ronald Saranchuk
Elaine Sartison (Brusnyk)
Debbie Sawchuk
Pat Sawchuk
Carol Scherban (Repka)
Richard Scherban
Ted Scherban
Zonia Schiewe (Zaharodny)
Jennifer Semchuk
Orest Semchuk**
Taras Semchuk
John Serink
Ron Shapka
Barrie Shewchuk
Robyn Rae Shewchuk
Sylvia Shewciw (Lytwyn)
Zen Shewciw
Ron Shymko
Richard Sliwkanich
Rosaline Sliwkanich (Kupchenko)
Ron Solowan
Kathie St. Arnaud (Zarsky)
Joyce Stach (Slade)
Joe Stanishewsky
Donna Stechishin
Tom Stefanyk*
Bohdan Stus
Bob Sulyma
Doreen Sulyma
Iris Sulyma
Lois Sulyma
Lorrie Sulyma (Maday)
Michael Sulyma**
Terry Sulyma
Lelia Sumka
Terry Sumka
Michael Taciuk
Larissa Talpash
Myron Tarnawsky
Joanne Ternovoy (Orlecki)
Daria Thew (Melnychuk)
Maryann Thornton (Hawryshko)
Dianne Trautwein (Kassian)
David Ungarian
Dianna Ungarian

Randy Ungarian
Maria van Steenoven (Hoermann)
Joanne Veroba (Bodnar)
Daria Wallsten (Iwansiw)
Daryl Warawa
David Warawa
Leonard Wasylynchuk
Levern Wasylynchuk
Howie Waye
Marsha Weleschuk
Myron Wintonyk
Gerry Wowk ☆
Loverne Wowk ☆
Odarka Wozniak (Pritz)
Marie Wujcik (Wolchansky)†
Darryl Yacey
Eugene Yakimishyn
Motria Yanda
Roman Yereniuk
Dennis Yurkiwsky
Orest Yusypchuk
Merv Zaddery
Gloria Zaharia (Holychuk)
Nada Zahorodny
Leo Zalucky*
Mary Zalucky (Hoshko)
Lisa Zorniak
Michael Zukiwsky
Olga Zukowski (Dmytruk)
Christine Zwozdesky (Faryna) ☆
Gene Zwozdesky**

CURRENT MEMBERS (1991)

Larissa Banting
Shelley Borowski
Stephen Burak
Lorraine Chanasyk ☆
Darka Cherkawsky ☆
Jason Chomik
Laurel Chomyc
David Conway
Kevin Hladunewich
Cherisse Killick
Ron Kopan
Kathy Kowalishin
Michelle Litvinchuk

Jennifer MacLean
Larissa MacLean
Larissa Makowsky
Dean Mazur
Teresa Manchak
Tracy Metrunec
Danny Niawchuk
Michael Orysiuk
Sheryl Passek
John Pichlyk ☆
Alana Prytuluk
Leda Prytuluk
Natalka Prytuluk
Doug Rachinski
Roxanne Rachinski (MacLean)
Maureen Safranovich
Erin Safronovich
Todd Safronovich
Nadine Samycia
Russ Samycia
Darvin Saskiw
Kevin Saskiw
Brian Shewchuk
Sandra Shewchuk
Scott Stefura
Taras Stefura
Viktor Stepovy
Catherine Storchuk
Darrell Sydora
Eunice Symak
Tom Syvenky
Wally Tarnawsky
Kathleen Todoruk
John Zinchuk ☆
Evan Zukiwsky
Greg Zukiwsky

** Honorary Lifetime Member
☆ Membership with Distinction
* Member, Founding Executive, Alumni Association
† Deceased

CHRONOLOGY OF
MAJOR PERFORMANCES

1959 Nov. 29 - Premiere Performance, UNO hall, Edmonton

1960 Feb. 7 - St. John's Cathedral Hall, Edmonton
          May 28 - Jubilee Auditorium, Edmonton
          Oct. 29 - Jubilee Auditorium, Harvest Festival

1961 Oct. 28 - United Nations 16th Anniversary Celebration Concert, Alberta College, Edmonton

1962 Mar. 2 - "Ukrainian Rhapsody," Jubilee Auditorium, Edmonton
          Mar. 30 - 30th Anniversary, Founding of the UNO hall, Edmonton
          Nov. - School of Agriculture, Vermilion

1963 Mar. - Taras Shevchenko Centenary, Winnipeg
          June 1 - Vegreville, Alberta
          July 14 - Opening of the Westlock Community Centre, Westlock, Alberta
          Sept. 8 - Ukrainian Day, Elk Island Park, Alberta

1964 Feb. 14 - 5th Anniversary Concert, Jubilee Auditorium, Edmonton
          May 30 - Jubilee Auditorium, Calgary
          Sept. 6 - Queen Elizabeth Theatre, Vancouver

1965 June 4 - 6th Annual Concert, Jubilee Auditorium, Edmonton
          June 5 - Jubilee Auditorium, Calgary

1966 Sept. 21 - *The Ukrainian Shumka Dancers incorporate under the Societies Act of Alberta*
          Sept. 23 - Jubilee Auditorium, Edmonton
          Oct. 21 - Jubilee Auditorium, Calgary
          Nov. - Vancouver Folk Arts Council/Alberta Folk Arts Council Festival, Queen Elizabeth Theatre, Vancouver

1967 Jan. 22 - 49th Anniversary Concert Celebrating Ukrainian Independence, Jubilee Auditorium, Edmonton
          July 28 - Hull-Edmonton Twinning Celebrations, Hull, Quebec
          Aug. 1–4 - Expo '67, Montreal

1968 Aug. 2–3 - Dauphin Ukrainian Festival, Dauphin, Manitoba
          Oct. 11 - Jubilee Auditorium, Edmonton (Ninth Annual Concert)

1969 Aug. - Tunis, Africa (International Folk Arts Festival)
          Nov. 21 - Jubilee Auditorium, Edmonton

1970 Feb. - Centennial Celebrations, Yellowknife, North West Territories

1971 Jan. 15–16 - Jubilee Auditorium, Edmonton (with Tommy Banks/Original Caste)
          Aug. - Dauphin Ukrainian Festival, Dauphin, Manitoba

1972 Mar. 2–3 - Jubilee Auditorium, Edmonton (with Alberta Ballet)
          April - Kobasa Kapers, Jasper, Alberta

1973 Mar. 1–3 - Jubilee Auditorium, Edmonton (with Stratus Faction)

1974 Mar. - Alberta College of Art, Calgary
          Aug. - Expo '74, Spokane

1975 Mar. 7–8 - Jubilee Auditorium, Edmonton
          Mar. 15 - Manitoba Centennial Centre, Winnipeg
          Apr. - Saskatoon

1976 Feb. - First Ukrainian Dancing Schools in Concert Performance, Jubilee Auditorium, Edmonton
          Aug. 1–22 - Hakone, Japan

1977 Mar. 2–4 - Jubilee Auditorium, Edmonton
          July 1 - Canada Day Celebrations, Ottawa
          Aug. - Hakone, Japan

1978	July 1	-	Canada Day Celebrations, Ottawa
	Aug. 1	-	Gala Performance for Queen Elizabeth II, Citadel Theatre, Edmonton
	Aug. 3	-	Opening Celebrations, Commonwealth Games, Edmonton
1979	Mar.	-	20th Anniversary Tour: Winnipeg, Saskatoon, Calgary, Edmonton, Hamilton, Detroit
	July 1	-	Canada Day Celebration, Ottawa
1980	Feb.	-	Symphony Pop Series, Edmonton Symphony Orchestra
	July 6–15	-	Calgary Stampede, Calgary
1981	Feb.	-	Symphony Pops Series, Edmonton
	Mar. 10	-	Gala in Honour of President and Mrs Reagan, National Arts Centre, Ottawa
1982	Feb. 13	-	Jubilee Auditorium, Edmonton
	Feb. 20	-	Jubilee Auditorium, Calgary
	Feb. 27	-	Queen Elizabeth Theatre, Vancouver
	Mar. 5–6	-	Hamilton Place, Hamilton, Ontario
	Mar. 7	-	O'Keefe Centre, Toronto
	Apr. 16	-	National Arts Centre (Gala Performance for Queen Elizabeth II, on the repatriation of the Canadian Constitution)
	June	-	Kiwanis International Festival, Minneapolis
	Oct.	-	Symphony Pops Series, Edmonton
1983	Feb. 10–14	-	Hong Kong Arts Festival, Hong Kong
	July	-	Universiade (World University Games), Edmonton
1984	Feb.–Apr.	-	25th Anniversary Tour: Edmonton, Calgary, Winnipeg, Saskatoon, Ottawa, Toronto, Vancouver
	May	-	Chester Kuc Concert (celebrating 35 years of teaching Ukrainian Dance)
	July	-	Calgary Stampede, Calgary
	July	-	Travel Alberta Tourism Show, Dallas, Texas

1985	Feb.	-	Alberta Tourism Promotion, Epcot Centre, Florida
	June 15	-	Garden State Festival, Holmdel, New Jersey
	July 1	-	Canada Day Celebration, Ottawa
	July	-	Dance in Canada Gala, Halifax, Nova Scotia
	Sept. 21–22	-	Gala Performance, Opening of Calgary Centre for the Performing Arts Calgary, (Broadcast by CBC-TV)
	Oct. 31– Nov. 2	-	Feature Artists, Calgary Philharmonic Series, Calgary
	Nov.	-	Grey Cup Banquet, Edmonton
	Nov. 15	-	National Tour Association Convention, Reno, Nevada
1986	July	-	Expo '86, Vancouver
	Oct.	-	Alberta Tourism Promotion, Japan
	Nov.	-	20th Anniversary, Folk Arts Council, Edmonton
1987	Feb–Apr.	-	Tour: Edmonton, Calgary, Toronto, Saskatoon, Winnipeg, Vancouver
1988	Feb.	-	Opening Celebrations, 1988 Winter Olympics
	Feb.	-	Olympic Arts Festival Performance, Calgary (with the Capella Banduristiv of Kyiv)
	Mar.	-	Seoul-Calgary Twinning Celebrations, Calgary
1989	Feb.	-	40th Annual NHL All-Star Game, Edmonton
1990	Mar.	-	Dance in Canada Awards Gala, Calgary
	Aug.	-	Ukraine Tour: Kyiv, Lviv, Ivano-Frankivsk, Moscow
1991	Feb-Mar.	-	Tour: Edmonton, Calgary, Winnipeg, Saskatoon, Toronto, Montreal

GLOSSARY OF UKRAINIAN TERMS

(Note: the following glossary does not include words that are used only once in the text or are defined in context)

arkan - Circle dance

bandura - A type of stringed instrument

basolia - Three-stringed cello

chortyky - Mischievous spirits

chumak (plural: *chumaky*) - Wagoners and traders common in Ukraine during the seventeenth to nineteenth centuries

chytalnia - "Reading club," an institution of Ukrainian village life in which peasants gathered to hear literate villagers read from newspapers and pamphlets.

fartukh - apron

hetman - A *kozak* leader

hopak - Dance originating with the *kozaky*, in which male soloists show off their prowess

hora - Dance originating in Romania

husli - Stringed instrument

hutsulka - Dance popular in the western mountains, combining features of the *kolomyika* and the *kozachok*

keptar (plural: *keptari*) - Vest typically worn by men and women in the mountain regions

khliboroby - Makers of bread

kobza - Stringed instrument, similar to the bandura

kolomyika - Circle dance in which individuals move to the centre and improvise movements

korsetka (plural: *korsetky*) - Vest typically worn by women in central Ukraine

kozachok - Dance originating in central Ukraine

kozak (plural: *kozaky*) - Cossack

mavka (plural: *mavky*) - Wood nymph

poias - Sash or woven belt

prysiadka (plural: *prysiadky*) - Dance step involving kicks done from a squatting position

rusalka (plural: *rusalky*) - Water nymph

sharavary - Wide pantaloons worn by men in central Ukraine and other regions

shtany - Narrow-legged pants typically worn by men in mountain areas

sich (plural: *sichy*) - Fortified centre, usually on an island, built by the *kozaky*

skomorokhy - Early semi-professional performers of music and dance

sopilka - A flute-like instrument

sorochka (plural: *sorochky*) - Shirt

torban - A type of stringed instrument

troisti muzyky - "The three musicians," the standard accompaniment for dance, always including a violin

tsymbaly - Dulcimer-like instrument

vinok (plural: *vinky*) - Wreath worn by unmarried girls

Zaporizhzhia - "Beyond the rapids," referring to the region inhabited by the Zaporizhzhian Cossacks in the area of the Dnipro River

zhupan - long-sleeved, knee-length coat